MAN OF THE FUTURE

Lazarev S.N.

MAN OF THE FUTURE

The First Step Into the Future

"Therefore, do not worry about tomorrow,
for tomorrow will worry about itself.
Each day has enough trouble of its own."

(Matthew 6:34)

Table of Contents

What Will a Person of the Future Be?

Early one morning, a man went into his field. He walked through it and carefully looked at the ground. He scooped up a handful of soil and rubbed it between his palms. He looked at the sky and at the trees beyond the field. He listened to the birds singing. In nature, everything is interconnected not only in the present, but also in the future. Are the frosts going to be severe this season? Has spring settled in well enough for planting seeds? The man recalled omens that were known to his father and grandfather before him. Omens are signs that connect the present and the future. There are certain days when the connection between the past and the future is especially strong. If on a particular day the weather is cold and gloomy, then the following spring might be as well. A mystical connection between past and future events definitely exists. For a human being this connection is destiny, or karma. The concept of karma can hold many lives, it shows how a person's thoughts and emotions correlate to his health and destiny, not only in the present, but also in the lives which follow.

In the Old Testament we are introduced to the idea of a connection between a parent's behavior and their children's destiny, revealed in allegorical form. The *"sin of the parents,"* or their improper behavior, is visited upon the children *"to the third and fourth generation"* (Exodus 20:5). This tells us that the universe exists in unity; that it is holographic not only in space but also in time. So if the future is inextricably linked to the present, then once we become detached from our shallow perception of the present we are able to foresee the future.

Let's start with a basic understanding of the law of cause and effect. A person sows seeds and hopes to harvest a crop in autumn. However, if the seeds turn out to be rotten, there will be nothing to harvest later on.

The person may diligently till the land and water it regularly, but the seeds will not sprout. Later, in autumn he will suffer, and during winter he will starve. If the man survives until the next spring he will borrow new seeds from somebody, but this time he will examine the seeds very carefully, as this present moment will determine his future.

Lets say that another man, the first man's neighbor, did not store food before the winter. He ate hearty meals, had fun, made merry and used up all his grain. His neighbors, knowing his character, will not lend him seeds. He is also capable of plowing and watering his field, but he has no seeds and harvesting a crop will be impossible for him this year.

Our behavior and attitude toward the world define what kind of crop we will harvest in the future. Any smart landowner, in order to not only survive but also prosper, must know the laws by which to influence and control the future through the present moment. The best seeds should be stored until spring. Seeds should not be damp and must be kept in a dry place. They should be planted, using omens, at the right time. The soil must be prepared, plowed and fertilized. Seeds must be planted at the right depth and at a correct interval from one another. We are now talking about the basic laws of cause and effect. The more clearly we see the connection between the past and the future, the more fully and precisely we can influence the present, and survive and evolve in the distant future.

Here is another story. Once, this same man planted his best seeds, having plowed his field, and did all of this with care and diligence. Still, a large part of the crop died for unexplainable reasons. The few bits that he was able to gather helped him survive during the winter. However, if not for the reserves he had saved earlier, his family might have died. The next year, he takes care of his future crop with more even greater diligence. The weather is favorable, and the crop turns out beautifully. However, when only a few weeks remain before harvest, the sky becomes covered in clouds, lighting flashes, and thunder rumbles. Heavy hail sweeps across his field, and the crop is destroyed. Again, what the landowner is able to gather is barely enough to survive.

However, it is necessary for him to live, to take care of his close ones, to save at least a few seeds for the upcoming year. And so next spring, the man once again walks out onto his field. He has borrowed some seeds to sow, and must have a nice crop come autumn or his family might not survive. A week remains before planting season, he has to pull his strength together, gather his sons for help, and begin determining the future through the present moment.

On the next morning the farmer gets out of bed, and suddenly his body is pierced by severe pain. He realizes that he is sick and will not be able to help his family. But that is not all – both of his sons are sick as well.

The man lies down on his bed and looks up at the ceiling. His future has collapsed; all of his efforts where in vain. At first he had some misfortunes in his life, and then real tragedies began. Now, they are not only around him but also inside of him. Suddenly, it dawns on him that his illnesses and misfortunes are also a harvest. Yes, it is possible to control the future by changing the outer world: selecting the best seeds, choosing the finest terrain, cultivating the land. However, it turns out that this is not what is most important. It turns out that our inner state is much more significant for our future, and the most important seeds are in our soul. The way our soul is, so will be our destiny. If the man's neighbor has a deformed soul, he will drink and revel away his harvest. Even if he comes to his senses, and, following the example of others, plants seeds and takes care of his field, his crop will die anyway.

The landowner stays in bed for one day and then another. He stops thinking about material things and his daily bread. His vague hypothesis, that his soul is related his destiny, grows clearer. The man looks around and realizes that he has begun to perceive the world differently. Beside him, he suddenly notices a Bible which he had overlooked before. With trembling hands, he takes the Bible, opens it at random and begins to read:

"If you walk in My statutes and keep My commandments so as to carry them out, then I shall give you rains in their season, so that the land will yield its produce and the trees of the field will bear their fruit.

Indeed, your threshing will last for you until grape gathering, and grape gathering will last until sowing time. You will thus eat your food to the full and live securely in your land.

I shall also grant peace in the land, so that you may lie down with no one making you tremble. I shall also eliminate harmful beasts from the land, and no sword will pass through your land" (Lev. 26:3-6).

Suddenly, the ill, decrepit man has an epiphany. He had constantly badmouthed and judged his good-for-nothing neighbor. He was always displeased with himself and his destiny, believing that his harvest was not large enough. He resented people who acted badly. Instead of sincerely telling them what he thought, and keeping them from improper behavior, he had become judgmental and angry.

The farmer puts the Bible aside and becomes lost in thought. Inside, he feels himself beginning to change. Once again, the man opens the Bible at random and begins to read. And incredulous, with tears in his eyes, reads:

"Ye shall not steal, neither deal falsely, neither lie one to another... Thou shalt not defraud thy neighbor, neither rob him: the wages of him that is hired shall not abide with thee all night until the morning. Thou shalt not curse the deaf, nor put a stumbling block before the blind... Thou shalt not hate thy brother in thine heart: thou shalt in any wise rebuke thy neighbor, and not suffer sin upon him. Thou shalt not avenge, nor bear any grudge against the children of thy people, but thou shalt love thy neighbor as thyself" (Lev. 26:11, 13-14, 17-18).

It turns out that the laws of spiritual connection are no less important than the laws of connection in the physical world. It turns out that the spiritual and physical are closely interrelated. The physical can influence the spiritual and can shape it. The spiritual can affect the physical and shape it. However, the spiritual is more important, and the physical is but an extension of the spiritual, an instrument in it's development.

Once again, the plowman looks around and notices with surprise that the world has become beautiful. He understands that he loves his wife, although before he had only reproached her and demanded obedience. He realizes how much he loves his children, whom he hadn't noticed before. All of a sudden, it dawns on him that he has begun thinking of his good-for-nothing neighbor as a silly child, neither judging him nor spoiling him with constant assistance. It is necessary to help not his body, but his soul first. So, the best way to help another person is by teaching them. In order to help the soul, the physical body should be at times indulged and at times restrained.

So that night, the man goes to sleep happy even though he has no future. He will not be able to plant seeds for the new crop, and he is unlikely to recover from his illness. But now, his daily bread is no longer the measure of his happiness. Now, he realizes how everyday worries about his material wellbeing had concealed his soul. Only now does he understand how unhappy he had been the past few years.

His soul had stopped singing, and the world had lost the refinement and subtleness of its colors. He had constantly convinced himself that a barn full of grain was the the best reason for happiness. Now, sick and dying, the plowman realizes that his soul had also reaped a harvest, but that in the past few years this harvest had been made up of indifference, resentment and greed.

When the soul suffers, there is a simple and dependable way to lessen its pain: by shifting one's attention to material things, convincing oneself that the main reason for happiness is money, material possessions, and sexual pleasure. If we forget about the soul, we stop noticing the soul's pain.

Sick and dying, the plowman remembers an old saying, "The gravest losses are those that we don't notice." He now understands that the most important happiness is the happiness of the soul. Despite the hopelessness of his situation, he goes to sleep happy. He sleeps calmly and peacefully that night, and the next morning, waking up, he notices with surprise that he feels much worse. The whole day, he can barely breathe because of acute, paralyzing pain. At the same time, however, something has changed. His misfortunes and losses, and even physical pain, no longer evoke feelings of despair, irritation, and discontent with his destiny. The pain makes him kinder and more forgiving. The pain forces him to forget about the physical body and turn to his soul.

While the body needs daily bread for its survival and salvation, the soul needs love. These seeds, bestowed by the Creator, are always pure and saving. The more the man suffered, the more love he felt towards God. The man was sick for a few more days, but began to feel better not only in his soul, but also physically. With surprise he noticed that his sons had also recovered, and realized that his wrong attitude towards the world had not only been destroying him, but also his own children. A week later, he went into his field once again and planted seeds together with his sons. Later, there were ill-timed frosts, and rains fell at the wrong moment, but regardless, the harvest turned out bigger and finer than the previous one, the crops were beautiful, there was not a single rotten seed.

Let's put this story aside, and return to today. Every spring, people continue sowing seeds in soil. Humankind has had success in things that need to be done in order to reap rich harvests. Every day we sow seeds of our destiny in our soul. I used to take great interest in books that spoke about people of the future. Now, many are curious about what people of the future will be like. But I have a different question, will there be a person of the future? Any person is a part of his society, and so in order for there to be a person of the future, our modern civilization must survive at the very least.

Three and a half thousand years ago, Jews began to meticulously follow the Ten Commandments given by God. They tried not to steal and plunder, not to worship money and sexual pleasure. They did not eat pork because this meat was considered impure, and was therefore harmful to the soul. If one of them had tried to visualize the kinds of people that would live one and a half thousand years later in the free Israeli nation, then, perhaps, a contemporary of Moses would have imagined them as "angels without sin." However, if we open the New Testament, we read about Christ casting demons out of a man and transferring them into a herd of swine. By the way, the pigs in that herd numbered more than 2000. Even according to our current standards, the herd was not small. This means that inwardly, people had already stopped following God's Commandments, and that this had begun to show outwardly through a disregard of the main Commandments. There was a serious crisis of belief in God, and Judaism as a whole. If a contemporary of Moses had tried to visualize what a person might be like in three and a half thousand years, he would have probably lacked imagination. However, let's suppose that miraculously, just for a moment, our ancestor could see the future. What would he have thought seeing the homosexual parades in modern Europe? Alternatively, what would he have thought if he saw the exuberant porn culture and persistent violence on today's television? Most likely, he would have thought he had gone insane.

"These people worship vices," he would have said. "They take pleasure in their own sinfulness and put it on display. Even their art doesn't purify the soul, but rather contaminates and damages it. These people have invented mechanisms and devices that have begun consuming them." It would be interesting to know what the prophet Daniel would have said about modern man. In order to speak about a person of the future, it is necessary to see this future. Who, if not the prophets, can speak about what a person of the future will be like?

There is an incredible foresight of the future through dream analysis as described in the Old Testament. The ruler of Babylon, Nebuchadnezzar, was very prosperous in his kingdom, and that prosperity obstructed his vision of subtle connections. He ordered the casting of a golden idol of huge proportions, and those who refused to worship this idol, he killed. He did everything he pleased, and nobody could oppose him. However, misfortune had already settled in his soul, and he began to see strange dreams from which we was unable to recover. These dreams predicted his future: the fall of the empire, the death of his children, and his own insanity. When the prophet Daniel interpreted these dreams for him, the king fell to his knees before him. However, habits cultivated over decades are very difficult to change instantaneously. When several people refused to bow to the golden idol, believing in One God, he ordered them thrown in the fire. The flames of the fire were so strong that they killed the servants who pushed the transgressors into the fire.

"But these three men, Shadrach, Meshach and Abed-nego, fell into the midst of the furnace of blazing fire still tied up. Then Nebuchadnezzar the king was astounded and stood up in haste; he said to his high officials: Behold I see four men loose, and walking in the midst of the fire, and there is no hurt in them, and the form of the fourth is like the Son of God" (Daniel 3:23-24).

The astonished king pardoned the men and showered them with favors.

However, just because a person recognizes a miracle, this doesn't mean that he has changed. In order for land to bear a good harvest, it is necessary to meticulously care for it. In order for the soul to bear a healthy harvest, we must care for it even more meticulously. The Bible depicts an incredible scene describing how Nebuchadnezzar's sins were passed onto his son, Balthazar, who inherited the kingdom. At the exact moment when Balthazar was throwing his greatest feast for thousands of his nobles, when the table was loaded with golden and silver vessels full of various provisions, just at this moment the king received testimony of his oncoming death.

While they drank and honored their golden and silver, copper and steel, wooden and stone gods, in the air near a lamp there appeared a human hand, and inscribed on the wall the following words: *MENE, MENE, TEKEL, UPHARSIN (Daniel 5: 25).* The astonished and frightened ruler called for the prophet Daniel, who explained the meaning of the words:

"God has numbered your kingdom's days and brought it to an end. You are weighed on the balances and found to be lacking. Your kingdom is divided and given over to the Medes and Persians" (Daniel 5: 26-28).

The ruler generously rewarded Daniel, sensing that he had told the truth and accurately foretold the future. On the same night, Balthazar, the Chaldean king, was slain.

While trying to envision a person of the future, we should first understand what he should not be like. We should imagine what society of the future should not be like; explore the mechanism of the fall of civilizations, understanding the connection between a person's soul and his destiny. It is necessary to outline the main dangers that can cross out the future of not only a single person, but all mankind. We must ask ourselves not what a person of the future might be like, but rather what he needs to be like in order to survive. Our harvest will depend on the kind of seeds we select, how we store them, and the soil in which we plant them. In order to envision what a person of the future will be like, we must look around at each other. We must understand what kind of people we need to be today in order to have a future tomorrow.

Chapter 1

The Kingdom of Heaven

In order to understand life, we need to first study the phenomenon of consciousness. Life and consciousness are inextricably linked to one other. When trying to understand consciousness we face a paradox. Any sensible person is aware that consciousness depends on social environment, that is, on purely physical factors. Not a single "Mowgli" has ever learned to speak. If in his first three years a child doesn't actively communicate with other people, he will not grow up to be a person. I remember an article that stated some fascinating facts. In Western Siberia hunters came across a child among a pack of wolves. They surrounded the pack, attempting to take the child. The wolves did not run away. Instead, they tried to protect the boy to the bitter end; all the wolves were killed. The little boy behaved completely like a wolf; he snarled and tried to bite the hunters. Unbelievably, even his bone structure had changed; he had begun to look like a wolf.

It appears that our genotype is not as stable as we had assumed. Earlier, scientists had believed that DNA is active only during fetal development. It has now been discovered that our core principal information actively interacts with the outer world throughout our entire life. Europeans who live in Asia begin to look like Asians. Spouses living in mutual harmony begin to resemble each other. The conclusion is clear: consciousness is formed by material factors.

In Russia, there were occasions when babies in orphanages did not receive the affection, emotional warmth, and interaction they needed during the first three years of their lives and became mentally retarded. Time had slipped away, and the physiological changes had become irreversible.

However, there is another side to this paradox. There is a large collection of facts in the world which prove the existence of consciousness after the death of the physical body. All religions recognize the existence of the soul, which continues to live after the death of the body. Science asserts that consciousness is a function of the physical body, the product of highly organized matter; the brain. Religion insists that the soul lives much longer than the body, and influences the physical body to a greater extent than scientists assume. It is possible to reconcile these seemingly incompatible contradictions if we concede that there are different forms of consciousness.

A tree grows out of a seed, and one can safely say that the seed is primary in relation to the tree. However, the seed comes from the fruit of a previous tree, and we can state with the same certainty that this tree is primary in relation to the seed. Again we face the same question: what is primary – consciousness or matter? This question can be answered if we agree that matter and consciousness are manifestations of the same substance.

By the way, the age old riddle of what came first, the chicken or the egg, has recently been solved. The conclusion made by geneticists was surprising. It turned out that the egg came before the chicken. The proof is very elegant: geneticists determined that the genotype of a living being doesn't change fundamentally during its lifespan. Superficial changes can occur, but the underlying structure remains unchanged. A new life form could only originate from an egg, so a chicken had to come from an egg laid by another living being. This fact makes us reevaluate the process of evolution.

Let's touch upon one of the most sensitive topics, the evolution of man. Before Darwin, the entire world was believed to have been created by God. The idea that living beings could change in future generations was inconceivable. Darwin was able connect isolated observations into a single system, and this system undeniably stated the following: if a type of living being is placed in new conditions, then its next generation will begin to change, and in time a new type of living being might appear. Darwin's conclusion is quite logical: the reason for the appearance of new life forms isn't God, but rather changes in the physical environment.

Modern scientific studies conclusively prove Darwin's theory. It turns out that every living being carries within itself the memory of previous generations. Therefore, not only external events are interconnected by an invisible thread. Treating ill patients, I saw again and again that when influencing the present, we simultaneously affect the future. By changing our attitude toward the past, we affect it. Affecting the past, we influence both the present and the future.

Lets remember the scene from the Gospels where a sick man approaches Christ. Illness is the result of sin - this was known in ancient India and is often referred to in the Old Testament. Suddenly, Christ utters a phrase blasphemous for his times, *"Your sins are forgiven."* (Matthew 9:5) Sins are actions in the past that have created illness in the present. This means that Christ could change a person's past. In India it would be said that Christ was able to burn stored up negative karma. He possessed the secret of governing time.

So, a person carries within him the memory of his ancestors, which means that the actions and sins of his parents can be passed onto him. That which healers call a curse over a family is also a fact. In my own healing practice, I often witnessed how generations of descendants suffered, agonized, and became ill if one of their ancestors committed a murder or a suicide; for example, if a woman did not want to live for a long time, or if she had a late-term abortion. However, it turns out that we carry within us not just the memory of the emotions and behaviour of our ancestors.

Scientists conducted an incredible experiment. In a state of hypnosis, participants were taken back into the state of childhood. Their pulse, breathing, blood and general physiological state were those of little children. Their thinking, and the level of questions and answers were also relevant to the level of children. The participants were then asked to describe what would happen to them in the future (which in reality was already the past for them). They willingly spoke about the schools they would graduate from, which colleges they would get into, where they would work, when they would get married, and how many children they would have. As the scientists had already obtained this information, they could easily verify that these facts fit.

Then the most interesting thing happened. In the state of hypnosis, the participants were asked to speak about what would happen to them in the real future. They talked about events that would take place in five and ten years. This information is unknown to all and therefore, cannot be confirmed. We just have to wait. So, events of the past and future are not isolated. They are a living, united chain. Affecting any period of time, we influence the whole of time altogether. Almost two thousand years after the birth of Christ, there appeared a man who understood that time could be influenced, and that patients could be treated in this way. This was Sigmund Freud.

He hypothesized that the past does not disappear, but is eternally stored in a person's subconscious. Therefore, if one changes a person's attitude to past negative events stored in his subconscious mind, it is possible to cure diseases. Freud tried this, and it worked. In fact, the method of psychoanalysis originated from this discovery. A situation forms emotions and creates illness. It turns out that consciousness is secondary. A disease is generated by the environment. However, using our consciousness, we can change our attitude to past situations, in this way affecting the past event and altering its code in our memory. This means that our consciousness becomes less dependant on the events in our past.

In the state of hypnosis, a person can convince himself that cold water is boiling hot, and he will get burned. However, under the same hypnosis, a person convinces himself that boiling water is in fact cold, and receives no burns. A Tibetan monk, sitting in a tub with boiling water, explained to passers-by, "You have convinced yourselves that this water is boiling, and you can get burnt, and I have convinced myself in quite the opposite." From a scientific point of view, this is not possible - the monk should have boiled long ago. We must conclude that it is consciousness that controls the outer world and can change the physical qualities of material objects.

Let's go back to Darwin's theory. A Human embryo comes into being as the simplest one- cell organism, living in water. The very act of conception repeats the moment of creation of life on Earth. Life, as information, impregnates the substance of the world's oceans. First, the simplest one-cell organisms appear, and then fish. A human embryo also originally has gills and a tail, and then it turns into a reptile, something like a lizard. In the process of evolution, he develops into a human being. So, a human being appears as a result of evolution. However, scientists have not yet found the missing link between monkeys and human beings. Therefore, many are now saying that Darwin's theory is not accurate.

There are only two points of view: either the theory is correct or incorrect. Let's try to solve this paradox. It is possible that man appeared over a short period of time, that is, the emergence of man happened within one or two generations. This would mean that Cro-Magnons, rather than giving birth to their own young, began giving birth to humans. This is similar to the way a chicken hatched out of an egg not laid by a chicken. This would mean that the information about this new form of being came from the future. So, it is necessary to recognize that time is not a homogenous, amorphous value. It consists of two currents flowing toward one another. On a subtle plane, they are a united whole. Then, it turns out that religion is right, claiming that man was created by a higher power, and Darwin, claiming that man emerged as a result of the evolution of other living beings, is wrong.

The main sign of life is consciousness. It consists of two parts. The first part is memory, which allows us to use our past experience: genetic memory, long term memory, and short term memory. The second component is the imagination, which modulates the future, and without which no living being can survive.

A human being differs from an animal in that he has a far greater memory of the past, and also possesses the ability to plan and modulate future events. If, due to a trauma, a person where to lose his memory of past events, he would become disabled. A person would become similarly handicapped if he was unable to modulate the future. Consciousness compresses time, pulling the past and the future into a single point. So what, then, is primary, spirit or matter? Matter, for us, is the past; spirit is the future. Both are functions of time, and and therefore appeared simultaneously. On the highest subtle plane, where the universe is united, all events that are about to happen have already happened. Meanwhile, on the outside, the past gradually flows into the future. It's possible to influence this process on subtle planes. There are various layers of the past, which pass into the future. Like a Russian Matryoshka, one layer hides under another.

Therefore, any event that happens is a complete sum of future and past, and unexplainable leaps in evolution can be explained quite easily. Packages of new information come from the future and fertilize the present moment. Then, the Big Bang theory, according to which the universe is cooling down after a Big Bang, is only partially correct. The universe is continuously receiving new informational packages; it is an actively evolving substance. In fact, the expansion of the universe confirms this. Therefore, the stars and planets, including our earth, are not burning and cooling cosmic bodies. The energy constantly coming from the future is necessary for the sun to shine and for the earth to expand. Time becomes energy and energy becomes matter. So, from this point of view, a person is a being that has a consciousness linked to the physical body and dependant on it, dissolving when the body dies. Simultaneously, a human being is a form of consciousness that determines the existence of the physical body, and continues to exist after the body falls apart.

Life appeared first as a form of consciousness. This universal consciousness impregnated the protein matter in the worlds oceans. In this way, life is an uninterrupted link between the past and the future. Consciousness, subtle energy fields, are the future. The physical body, matter, is the past. There is a well-known saying: "Man is the master of his fate". This means that using his will, his consciousness, a person can affect his destiny and future. There is also an equally just saying, "Destiny is the ruler of man." This means that the subconscious, in which information is stored about the past and future, affects man just as much.

Mankind always tried to find out about its future. Every ruler always had mystics, astrologers, seers, and fortune tellers present at court. Many years ago, in ancient India, clear ideas about the future developed: the future as unchangeable, inevitable, and impossible to influence. Centuries passed and people evolved. In Judaism, time was understood as a slightly different value. It turned out that with our behaviour we affect the future, and the sins we have committed in the past, bring us illness and misfortune not only in the present, but also in the future. Our past sins are paid for by our children, grandchildren and great-grandchildren. However, if a person turns to God and repents, then the pardoning of sins is possible. That is, changing the present and the future is possible.

The laws of Manu, who in India is considered to be the ancestor of all mankind, do not talk about repentance. For every crime there is supposed to be a punishment. However, in Judaism even a punishment sent from above can be annulled through re-evaluation of past events and repentance.

In Christianity, the future is already perceived in a completely different way. It is a physical substance, with which it is possible to interact. It turns out that the future can have it's own distinctive characteristics and qualities. It turns out that a person actively interacts with the future, which has a completely different structure from the present. When a person comes in close contact with this new future, he may even die.

In Indian philosophy, the past smoothly flows into the future. Everything is predestined, and the Creator doesn't interfere with current events. In Judaism, God interacts with people, and forces them to change their tangent of behaviour. Observing the Commandments allows a nation to survive and transform its future. In Indian philosophy, disease is the result of a person's behaviour, and therefore, there is no point in trying to cure it. One must suffer through one's stored up karma. In Judaism, disease is also a result of accumulated sins, but through prayer, repentance and fulfillment of the Commandments, it is possible to remove sins, bettering one's future and the future of one's descendants. Christianity stops looking back at transgressions that a person committed in the past. Through intense love for God and inner change, it is possible to overcome any negative past. So, suffering as a means of repentance is not what is most important, nor strict observance of the Commandments and repentance as a way of changing the past. Rather, it is an intense love for God as a way of changing the past and the future. Then a question appears: what should a person be like, in order to come into contact with the new future? And why can a person die from contact with it?

A person can live observing all of the Commandments given from above. However, when the new future comes, he still might die. That is to say, fulfilling the many Commandments and behaving righteously are not the codes of entry into the future that is approaching us. People who believe in God, fasting and trying to observe all of the proper religious dogmas, might still die when the new epoch and age approaches. The only ones who will be able to survive are those who carry within themselves the secret password for survival in the new future. Christ found a path of salvation for the sake of which, as it turned out, all of the rules and Commandments had been created. This is love.

A lit candle is standing in front of me on the table. I spend a long time looking at it, trying to put my thoughts and feelings in order. I then turn my gaze to the window. It's springtime in Berlin. The green leaves on the trees create an indescribable atmosphere and birds are joyfully singing. I had a session with with a patient today. People come for this from all over the world. Their life stories are different and often confusing. I speak with each one, and together we gradually untangle the events in their lives. I explain how thoughts, feelings and actions in their past have affected their health, character and destiny, and not only their own, but also those of their children and grandchildren. When you enter subtle planes and see that which is called a person's soul, it is immediately possible to make conclusions about his destiny several decades into the future.

Today I saw a married couple from Greece. They told me an interesting story. Their relatives have lived in Greece for a long time, own several houses, a thriving business, and big bank accounts. Recently, they invited their nephew from Kiev for a visit. The young man had grown up in poverty and was in need of everything. He was seventeen years old and the couple had no children.

The young man was good and kind and the family quickly became attached to him. They asked him to stay and live with them in Greece, and he gladly agreed. They promised to leave him all their property as inheritance: their homes and money. There was only one condition: that he stay with them in Greece and never leave them. A year later, he asked for their permission to go back home for a couple of weeks to see his parents and his city. During this trip, something unexpected happened - he fell in love and immediately became seriously ill. The relatives begged him to return as soon as possible and begin treatment, but he was physically unable to do so. Two weeks later he phoned them and said that he refused to accept the inheritance and did not want to live in Greece.

"So what happened then?" I asked.

One of the spouses shrugged. "He stayed in Kiev. For some reason, he decided that he had become ill because he lived in Greece. So, one of the reasons we came here was to find out what had happened to him."

"You want to know if he was right or not?" I asked.

The man looked at me searchingly and nodded. "Of course."

"You know, children's souls are purer than those of adults. They are usually not covered by layers of superiority, self defense and self confidence. Therefore, they feel love more clearly and sense the dangers that lie in wait for love. If he had fallen in love not at eighteen, but at the age of twenty or twenty-three, he would probably have died. He had no antidote to the sudden wealth that had swept over him and which he had not earned.

The secret of good health and happiness is actually very simple. You give away a portion of love and energy, and receive approximately the same amount of health, money and other forms of happiness. If you give away five times more energy than you receive money and well being, then you will have stable health and happiness, and an unexpected influx of money and good fortune will not kill you. If you have gained or desire to gain several times more than you have given, then you are ill. You will no longer own this wealth; rather, the wealth will own you.

So, when the young man came to Greece and gained everything he had wished for, without much effort, his soul began imperceptibly dying. He did not have a tuning fork to give him a sign when his soul wandered. However, when he experienced love, all of the inner dirt came out. The soul was purified and the dirt passed on to the body; for this reason he became ill. Many people who do not come in contact with real love can live for a long time happily and plentifully. Even when they lose the ability to internally love and give energy, they continue to live in total comfort.

The tragedy is that a person can run away from love in order to live comfortably. If one concentrates on external happiness, on its material aspects, it is possible not to notice the death of the soul. However, if this person has children, then they will still have to encounter love. And then all that the children aren't able to stand, their parents will bear, and will do so for more than one life. The soul is not a one time concept.

Not only a person, but also a government can behave in this same way. It's possible to teach our children a condescending and flippant attitude towards love. Love can be equated with sexual relationships. One can convince oneself that love can be used for control. Then already several generations of our descendants will run away from love.

But sooner or later this government and society comes into contact with this feeling, coming from the future. The higher the dam shielding people from love, the more lamentable the consequences will be for those who try to protect themselves from it. So, this young man felt and realized that one must be defenseless in the face of love, and threw away everything that gave him protection. Why does unearned money kill? It kills because there is more consumption in it than return. A person who wants to receive more than he gives begins to degenerate.

Why do the stars shine? They shine because they want to be happy. Giving energy is happiness not only for animate but also for inanimate beings. On the subtle plane, animate and the inanimate beings feel and react identically. Whether we receive externally or give, inside there must always be a release of the energy of love. We receive a gift and rejoice, and this is a release of energy. We give a gift to somebody and also rejoice, and this is an even greater release of energy. This is a universal law.

I recently read a story about a king who lived during the Middle Ages. He traveled disguises as simple knight, and once became lost and sought shelter. Only in one house was he made welcome. The king then revealed his true name and said that he would assign a high-ranking title to the person who had opened his doors to him. Suddenly, the man standing in front of him hesitated. 'I beg your pardon, your Majesty, but you do not know my profession.' he said. 'I never reverse my orders,' said the king without flinching. 'Name your trade.' 'I am an executioner,' the man replied.

The king did not reverse his decision. The man who had let him into his house received a title, and with it, material rewards. The king was right to do this because in reality, this person who worked as an executioner did not kill anybody. He performed his duty and helped victims to go to the next world with minimum anguish. High ranks are given for feats performed by subjects. At the heart of every feat is self-sacrifice, and the sense of love without which real sacrifice is not possible. The man who worked as an executioner demonstrated this ability to sacrifice and love.

Whatever situation our destiny puts us in, whatever role we perform, we do not have the right to refuse God our love. The loss of this feeling is the beginning of all other transgressions. We are only able to have wealth and happiness to the point where they begin to interfere with our ability to love, to sacrifice, and to give energy. A person who knows how to love always intuitively stops at the line beyond which wellbeing will begin killing him, abandoning the wealth that has begun to destroy his soul."

Memories take me to events two decades earlier. For a few years, I worked as an artist-designer in a cultural center not far from the world famous Mariinsky Theatre, in St. Petersburg. Later, this cultural center closed, and I began a period of 'swimming free.' I would not have started to practice healing seriously if I had had a job, because I already sensed that it was a dangerous profession. It turned out that the situation itself pushed me to experiment. Besides, I remembered the words of Hippocrates, "A physician-philosopher is Godlike," and decided to try connecting philosophy and medicine. It was then that I first noticed with surprise that if a person's body was sick, this was often linked with a disease of the person's soul and destiny.

A friend of mine once said, "We have a proverb in the East, 'Material loss always comes before disease.'" I remembered that we have a similar saying in Russia, "When troubles arrive, keep the gates open." Why does a person's destiny come ill and crumble? Which causes lead to sickness of the soul? Why do shortcomings in a person's character lead to illness? Back then, I did not know the answers to these questions.

I once again return to the present. It is spring 2007. There are many signs that indicate the approach of new portions of our future. We've gotten used to the fact that the present smoothly flows into the future, shaping it, and we don't see the reverse process. However, occasionally, the future acts like a spring, actively invading the present. Then the old world crumbles, yielding space to the new.

There are several theories explaining the extinction of the dinosaurs. One of them is such: a meteorite landed and the conditions of survival on Earth abruptly changed. The same approach is used to explain the origin of man: if it is impossible to find the transitional stage between a monkey and a human being, then the explanation is as follows: aliens came to our planet from outer space and gave a beginning to a new kind of living being, humans. If a situation is inexplicable, one must admit the possibility of an outside influence. The easiest example is outer space, and all inexplicable occurrences are written of to it.

For example, the expansion of our planet is explained by scientists as happening due to the large number of falling meteorites. Even though this explanation defies common sense, official science stubbornly clings to this theory, simply because of its lack of other hypotheses. To this day, science claims that the Earth is a cooling celestial body, because this concept corresponds to the theory of Kant-Laplace and fits into the familiar picture of the universe.

It is enough to conduct a simple experiment to understand that this theory has a serious flaw. Put a kettle on a gas stove. Wait until the water boils and the lid starts to bounce, then turn off the gas and return to the kettle in five minutes. If the lid is still rattling and steam is breaking out from under it, you will be very surprised because there can be no active processes in cooling bodies.

So if you believe the basic laws of physics, then the Earth should have no earthquakes. This "kettle" has been cooling down for five billion years, and if we forget the fear of a collapsing paradigm, we must recognize the simple truth: the Earth is not a cooling body. Earthquakes and volcanic eruptions confirm this. Moreover, our planet is now entering a period of increased instability. Energy is coming to the Earth from outside. The fifteen cubic kilometers, by which our planet increases each year, also do not adhere to the theory of meteor showers. Even a child can understand that the mass of our planet is growing not on the outside but from within. Falling meteorites cannot force continents to move apart. Thus, the use of the space factor is most likely a clumsy attempt to explain the unexplainable. If, however, you introduce a factor called the 'future,' then everything falls into place.

I remember how stunned I was when I saw that a person can subconsciously react to future events. "How strange," I thought. "The event has not yet happened, yet the person has already reacted to it." Then I saw that many diseases in children are related not to the past, but to the future, that is, illness is a form of adaptation to future events. However, if a person reacts to the future, this means that the future exists, it is a physical value with which it is possible to interact. Then, inexplicable changes in the present can be understood as the strengthening influence of the future on the now. Why did dinosaurs become extinct? Because they started to bring completely new beings into the world. That is, 'chickens' began to hatch from dinosaur eggs, and Cro-Magnons suddenly started giving birth to people, whose characteristics corresponded to the new time.

So, the new time is different to the old. If a person does not correspond to the energy of the future, he simply is not going to survive. How are the characteristics of present space, energy, and time different from the characteristics of these categories in new portions of the future that will possibly arrive soon? If we rely on our habitual paradigm, then the universe is the result of the Big Bang, and is gradually cooling down, losing its primary impulse. Then, a new portion of future should be weaker than what is in the present. If we hypothesize that the universe is an actively developing organism, then we should allow that there are opposite processes in the universe: in addition to the slowly fading ones there must be actively intensifying ones.

So, will the future be weaker or stronger than the present? I recall a brief article in a newspaper. People have been watching the sun for the past two hundred and thirty years, and always the eleven year phase of 'active' sun was followed by a similar phase of 'quiet' sun. There have been no exceptions to this rule. The sun evenly and quietly 'breathes,' obeying the universal rhythms. However, it seems that last year something inexplicable happened for the first time. The phase of 'active' sun, having ended, passed not into a quiet phase, but into an even more active one. Simply put, new energy has begun to come from somewhere, and the sun is trying to adapt to it.

It is possible that the new portions of the future will have much higher energy. This means that the only people who will be able to survive will be those with a high level of energy exchange. It appears that current 'dinosaurs' will become extinct. When does an average person demonstrate an increase in energy exchange? When he is in a dangerous or fatal situation. When he sees and understands that he is in danger. Exchange of energy increases when a person acts or works intensely. Exchange of energy is enhanced when we want to help or care for someone. Energy erupts when we fall in love.

From all of this, we can make a simple and elegant conclusion. To prepare present humankind for the future, there needs to be a series of disasters in which people will face death and find themselves in mortal danger. Then people will begin to care for one another, help each other overcome the consequences of these disasters. Then each day will be perceived by many as their last. This will break the chains that bind people to wellbeing and stability. People will be able to feel love once again, and this will help them overcome their attachments. There is another period in people's lives when they have very high energy, when they love incessantly, constantly rejoice and give energy away. This is childhood. If we maintain the potential for love and energy inherent in our childhood, then we have a chance to survive in the new future.

I open the Bible and see a passage that used to be completely incomprehensible to me:

"People were bringing little children to Jesus for him to place his hands on them, but the disciples rebuked them. When Jesus saw this, he was indignant. He said to them, "Let the little children come to me, and do not hinder them, for the kingdom of God belongs to such as these. Truly, I tell

you, anyone who will not receive the kingdom of God like a little child will never enter it." (Mark 10:13-15)

This scene is followed by the description of a strange episode:

"As Jesus started on his way, a man ran up to him and fell on his knees before him. "Good teacher," he asked, "what must I do to inherit eternal life?" (Mark 10:17)

Let's reflect on this passage. What is goodness? It is the absence of sin. We have become used to calling stability and material security goodness. However, real goodness is the energy of love. A good man is one in whom sin is completely absent . Translated into everyday language, the scene reads like this: a man comes up to Jesus and says: "You are sinless, so you will survive in the upcoming new time. What can I do to become as sinless as you are?" He wants to become one, to fuse into the Savior.

All of a sudden, Christ unexpectedly replies, *"Only God is sinless! In order to survive, we must rely first and foremost on ourselves."* Neither faith in Christ nor pleas for salvation can help if a person does not make an independent step. If you yourself do not want to feel the Divine within, nobody can help you.

Christ explains how it is possible to save yourself. Rule number one: turn to love, and therefore live in such a way for love to open up rather than departing from your soul. Do not commit adultery, do not to kill, do not steal, do not bear false witness, do not offend, honor your parents. Rule number two: maintain complete inner vulnerability. In order to come in contact with the Kingdom of God and stay alive, it is necessary for your soul to be free of aggression. Aggression is a form of protection. If we have nothing to defend, we will not have aggression. When a person has wealth, stability and security, this wellbeing gradually penetrates the soul. And if the pleasure derived from the possession of material goods is stronger than the pleasure derived from love, then the soul of such a person inevitably becomes more and more aggressive, and he will die when he encounters love.

We come to know God through the feeling of love, and when facing this feeling we must be completely defenseless. Again I recall the phrase of Jesus Christ, *"Children, how hard it is for those who trust in their wealth to get into the kingdom of God!"* (Mark 10: 24). What we hope for, we strive for. That which we strive towards for a long time becomes the main purpose of our existence. If a person's major goal is wealth as a form of protection of his physical body and instincts, his soul will begin to gradually lose love. A person with an empty soul has no future; his physical body is certainly doomed. Children are vulnerable, and this helps them to maintain love. The fact that in Western countries children no longer respect their parents and may even file a lawsuit against them proves the simple point: many people in the west already have no future.

I try to drive these thoughts away, and memory takes me once again to events that happened two decades ago. I remember my small office in a dusty street near the Baltic Railway Station where I began to see my first patients. Every session is a performance. It is necessary to unite every externally unrelated event in a person's life, compress them into the 'seed of a role.' I explain to my patients how illness appears as a result of protracted resentment, how problems of the soul pass on to the body and produce diseases, how the worship of material values brings forth misfortunes, and how the worship of a loved one leads to jealousy, resentment and divorce.

There were some cases that were unusual. I will tell you about one of them. One day a woman came to me and asked me to see her son.

"What are his problems?" I asked.

She looked at me a little strangely and then said, slowly, "He has mental problems."

"Where is he now?"

"At the Military Medical Academy, in the Department of Psychiatry," the woman paused, then added, "I will talk to the doctors so that they release him for a day." Then she glanced at me and asked, "What should he do before he comes to see you?"

I shrugged. "Nothing, really. He can stop by the church, especially since it is nearby."

The woman looked at me strangely again. "Better not, he should come and see you directly"

"When he comes tomorrow, let him be completely sincere," I added. "We'll compare what I see with what he will tell me."

The next day, he came. A young man of medium build sheepishly walked into the room and sat down in the chair in front of me. His face expressed nothing and his gaze was completely extinguished. Apparently, the doses of medicine he was taking were enough for a horse. The treatment had not been successful, so they had come to me.

"Please tell me everything in order from the very beginning," I said.

For a long time, he stared blankly into space. Then his eyes brightened and became meaningful. "There were sorcerers in our family," he began his story. Then he looked at me and anticipating the question, continued, "On the paternal side. My father had strong energy and a great ability to hypnotize." He looked at me and sensing the next question, replied, "I had nothing like that. I was a normal average child." His face clouded, and he again stared blankly into space. "At the age of eighteen, I was drafted into the army. I served in Afghanistan. You know how it was there. The atmosphere was terrible. There, I tried drugs for the first time, and I liked it. And then ..." He paused. The pause grew longer.

"Then you started having psychological problem, and got sick?" I suggested.

He slowly looked at me and shook his head. "No, my health was excellent, and my head was clear. However, something had happened to my mind, as if it had moved aside. My perception of the world changed somehow." He again became lost in thought. I could see that it was hard for him to speak.

"Once I was at my post, and that's when it started. There was a field next to the post. We were not allowed to walk on the field. However, there was a hole in the fence, and you could use it to take a shortcut. Many, no longer paying attention to the guards, used it to run their errands. Once, standing on guard, I saw how someone was once again trying to climb over the fence and dive into the hole. I felt irritation towards the man, and mentally commanded him, 'Fall! Fall onto the barbed wire and scratch yourself!' And it all happened exactly as I had thought."

"So," he continued, still deep in thought, "from that moment all of my wishes began coming true. Let's say there was a man walking in front of me and carrying two bags of empty glass bottles and jars. In my mind, I commanded him: 'Fall!' He immediately fell to the ground."

The young man, recalling the scene, unwittingly smiled. "He lay on the ground, screaming, understanding nothing, all of the bottles were broken. And whomever i mentally commanded, all of my orders were fulfilled." He again became grim and pensive.

"Then it became much worse. I noticed that my orders could be extended not only to other people."

He looked at me and continued, "Yes, I could command inanimate objects and the surrounding natural environment. I realized that I could control the weather and all events around me. The most interesting thing was that my abilities did not diminish; instead, they only grew. I needed only to think it, and a wish would come true."

"And how were you psychologically?" I asked with curiosity.

He shrugged. "I was still fine, and my physical health was excellent. However, something wrong began to happen to my soul. A sense of huge superiority over other people appeared. Whatever I did, I felt completely righteous. I noticed that I was degrading people more and more, and that this pleased me. I then decided to go to church in order to slow down this process in any way possible. I confessed to the priest that in my soul there was a growing anger and desire to humiliate and subjugate people. The priest said that he would recite prayers, and that I must stand by his side. Then, while reciting the prayer, he took me into the altar. Something happened at that moment. It was as if I had been broken inside. I left the church in a terrible state. I had never felt so bad before. My psyche started collapsing. I came home, but still felt very bad. I somehow made it to the evening, hoping that after a good night's sleep, the problem would go away. I remembered that the priest had advised me to put the Bible under my pillow. I did this. That night I slept more or less peacefully. However, upon waking, I noticed that I could not lift my head. There was unbearable heaviness and pain in my head. I had a feeling that all night my head had rested not on a pillow but on an anvil, and someone had been striking it with a hammer."

He paused again, and then waved his hand. "Yes, I've remembered that as I passed into the alter, I had a feeling of indescribable longing, and this pain in my soul did not go away. The next day I was in complete despair. Then I decided to pray. Immediately, all of the windows in the apartment swung open and a strong wind began to blow. A few minutes later the sky became covered with clouds and a heavy, a prolonged downpour began, followed by the thunder and lightning."

"Did you try to pray after that?" I asked with curiosity.

He shrugged his shoulders again. " I tried, but each time it was the same. I then felt that I could no longer stand this intense anguish, realized that I had mental problems and that treatment was necessary."

I looked at him and thought, "He is still one of few. What will happen to mankind if people like him are born more often?" I remembered the words of the genius inventor, Nikola Tesla, "The level of my technical capabilities is now so high that I can destroy the Earth."

Events of even earlier times surface in my memory; when I worked as a tourist guide. Once I found myself in a group of people who were all trying to recall interesting stories. One of the narrated events occurred in approximately 1900. Back then, in Russia there was an inventor who was mysteriously murdered.

After this, his apartment was searched, and all of his documents disappeared into the archives of the Tsarist secret police. This man had claimed that he had invented a device which emitted various wavelengths. It is well known that every object, animate and inanimate, generates its own waves, and by resonating with them, it is possible to affect the object, change its structure, recreate or destroy it. The sun also generates waves. "Now I can destroy the sun, and I have the proof," claimed the man. A few days later he was killed.

I looked at the young man sitting in front of me. "We wanted to develop our abilities," I told him, "and forgot that first of all it is necessary to develop our feeling of love and take care of our soul. Love is a car's driver, and abilities are the engine. With a powerful engine, and an inexperienced driver, the chances of survival are close to a zero. You had practically no chance of survival with your abilities. You were saved by your visit to the church. If you had came there later, you could have died right in the altar. Now, your abilities are tied down. You need to learn how to love. Your parents should remove all of their resentments towards each other from the time before your conception. Your mother especially needs to work, because she was critical of her husband during pregnancy. Every person has energy in their soul, most of it must be returned to God, and the smaller portion should go towards spiritual and physical strength. If we, forgetting about love, stop caring for the soul, then there is a sharp increase of material prosperity, abilities, and the like. We rejoice at the surge of money and fulfilled wishes, unaware that this robs our soul, and that we will repeatedly pay of this 'happiness' with our soul's anguish and the decay of our physical strength. Christ said that it would be difficult for the rich to get into the kingdom of God. Material wealth is a great temptation. However, spiritual security is far more treacherous. That is why Christ said: "Blessed are the meek." Many people, through fasts, sexual abstinence, and solitude, dramatically increase their spiritual possibilities. They develop powers and become clairvoyant, often without understanding that spiritual wealth is even more tempting than material wealth. Then the natural process where whatever we worship is destroyed begins. Abilities, spirituality and consciousness are the same sort of phenomena. If we worship them, they begin to subordinate us, make us slaves, and in order to save our souls, God takes away our abilities and consciousness."

I never met the young man again. His parents told me that after our conversation, he began to feel better. Hopefully, he can pray now.

The events of the past again spread out in a golden mist. I once again return to the topic of the approaching future. As different as it might be from our present, on the subtle plane everything is united, and often in order to foresee the future, we must analyze the past. In order for a misfortune not to repeat in the future, we must understand why the misfortune happened in the past. There's a simple principle: the more illogical the misfortune or tragedy that has happened, the more confusing and unpredictable it is, the more likely that higher powers have interfered.

When a person is showered with misfortunes out of the blue, his first thought should be that God has sent this punishment! If the person is an atheist, an unbeliever, then it is possible to assume that he is being punished for this. The way you relate to the Creator, so the Creator relates to you. However, if the person believes in God, what is he being punished for? If he follows the commandments and behaves ethically, then why does he get sick and have misfortunes?

I recall a question asked by a woman at one of my seminars.

"Can the Armenian genocide that occurred in 1915, when over a million people were killed, be explained from a divine point of view?"

"Let's try to figure this out," I replied. "The Armenians adopted Christianity in the III century of our era, that is, before the appearance of Islam. Faith in God fosters love in the soul, and love reveals itself as high spirituality, sensuality, and great material possibilities. Love is the foundation, and increasing possibilities and wealth are walls.

Now imagine that a foundation is built for only three stories. The owner starts to build a first floor, then a second and sees that his material happiness is becoming more and more full and grand. He forgets that he can build only three stories, and builds a fourth, fifth, sixth. Afterwards, the house must collapse and bury its owner beneath it.

Accordingly, people who do not believe in God should live in huts. In current primitive tribes the concept of love and morality have not yet fully developed, like the belief in a single God. As long as they live in shacks, this outlook is painless for them. However, if they come into contact with modern civilization, they begin to rapidly die out."

Now lets remember if there were other events in the history of mankind similar to the Armenian genocide. First, there was the extermination of the Jews, which began in ancient Egypt. Why did the Pharaoh order the killing of all Jewish male infants? He saw that their population had increased; that they had begun to pose a threat. The Pharaoh feared for his own security. But the victim and the perpetrator are always similar to one another. If a thief steals someone's money, this means that the victim has the same problems, but deep inside. The Jews' sense of increased security increased their subconscious aggression, provoking the Pharaoh's outward aggression. Physical security in the form of material prosperity can obscure love. Spiritual security is even more dangerous in this case.

In simple terms, a sense of righteousness and superiority is the source of future misfortunes. However, there is something still more terrifying. It is the security of the soul. This appears when a person comes to know the laws that control the universe. For thousands of years, Jews diligently studied the Torah, soaking up a correct attitude towards the surrounding world with their mother's milk: do not be envious, do not lie, do not steal, do not plunder, and do not kill.

For hundreds of thousands of years they saw how people who followed the Commandments were able to survive, while envious, greedy, and lustful people became ill and where wiped out. If they themselves were able to survive, their children got sick and perished. The Jews had received instructions for survival. Knowledge of the mechanism of cause and effect in the universe, as well as the laws of the soul, is tremendous wealth. The knowledge that an unwell soul breeds physical illnesses and misfortune is huge capital. But this security can obscure one's vision of the Divine. Many believers sincerely began to think that God was obligated to protect them if they observed all of the commandments. The feeling of being God's chosen people appeared in this way. So, the Commandments and rituals became the goal, and the Creator become the means. However, security and love are incompatible.

The idea of absolute superiority, security from above, was taken by the Nazis, who proclaimed, "God is with us!" They eliminated around six million Jews, and later were themselves destroyed. Why was Prometheus punished from above for helping people? Because by giving people the divine fire he made them more secure. No wonder there is a Russian proverb, "Until thunder begins to rumble, a man will never cross himself." It is at a moment of the surrounding world's destruction and our own complete vulnerability that we seek protection through oneness with eternity.

Fulfilling the divine Commandments we connect to love and eternity, and notice that our soul and body begin to recover. But as soon as we think that the Commandments and our rituals protect us, we lose sight of the main reason why these commandments exist: our feeling of love and unity with God. Then suddenly misfortunes and illnesses begin to rain down on believing, very spiritual people.

The Divine does not require protection because it is eternal. If the soul asks for security, this means that it has already lost unity with the Divine. It has lost its sense of eternity, and therefore must defend itself in order to survive. We know that a much greater opportunity for love, sensuality, wish fulfillment and accumulation of material wealth opens in a believing person and his descendants. However, few know that a believer's feeling of responsibility towards love is much higher than in others, and that a believer is punished more severely than others for the loss of love.

Why does one of the main Commandments state, "Do not bear false witness?" It seems clear enough: often we lie for our own benefit. Therefore one should not lie, because then one's focus on material gain will lead to disease and trouble. However, let us think about what bearing false witness really is. It is insincerity, and insincerity closes the soul. That is, it increases its defenses. Sincerity makes the soul defenseless and therefore makes it vulnerable to pain and pushes it towards love.

A person can conceal his thoughts but must not hide the feelings in his soul, because the hiding away of an emotion is its suppression, and suppression of a feeling makes the soul aggressive. For this reason, an insincere person is always aggressive inside. The more actively a person hides from emotional pain, the faster he loses the feeling of love. The more sincere a person is inside, the more pain he can experience, and the more intensely he must turn to love and believe in God. It was about these people that Christ said, *"Blessed are the pure in the heart: for they shall see God."* (Matthew 5:8)

Any event unfolds in time, like a wave. An event that must happen is already invisibly present in the present moment. If we react to early signs incorrectly, we may fail a future challenge while still not guessing at its existence.

I often I saw the following picture. A person is about to receive a huge portion of happiness. This may be the money that he will earn, a house that he will build, abilities that will develop in him and bring him respect and fame, or the love that he will feel for a woman. Before rewarding a person with something, God first checks to see whether he is able to sacrifice. Anyone who cannot lose has no right to gain. Then, instead of happiness, the person faces sickness or death.

Any experienced coach will never allow an unprepared athlete to participate in a competition. So, the very first wave that comes from the future interacts with our soul and our feelings. If the soul is aggressive, then instead of happiness in the future one might face disease, loss or death. This is because our most important choice is made not at the level of our body, mind, or spirit, but in the very depths of our soul, where the Divine becomes human.

"The Kingdom of Heaven is coming to us," I think. "Rumors of the end of the world have turned out to be not without reason. The impulse of the time in which we live seems to have used up its power, and the impulse of a new time is not far away."

"Life works in such a way that form crumbles and goes into the past, and content creates a new form, maintaining continuity with the old. Those who value form over content will remain in the past. Said more simply, those will survive who learn how to love."

Chapter 2

Mysticism

Soon it will be time for a telephone consultation. Before this, I close my eyes and renounce everything. For some reason, a vision comes of how a soul enters into the world. It is not the body or the mind of a person that comes into contact with the Creator, but his soul. If our souls do not periodically return to their Source, they gradually lose their higher energy. They forget the feeling of higher love: the higher pleasure derived from union with God, which at the same time is their source of higher energy. Our souls begin to empty, to weaken, and then our physical bodies degenerate.

I wonder why the souls of extraordinary children come to us through the center of the Sun. In my memory a picture comes up, prior to conception. A lonely soul, sparkling and shimmering, comes into our world from other worlds. It takes less then an hour for the soul to pass through the center of the sun, pausing there. Then for some time the soul floats around the Sun, and, only after about two or three weeks, approaches Earth. For some time, the soul rests around the South Pole, then flits around the Earth, again returns to the South Pole and begins a slow descent to Earth.

For about a year, the soul stays near the future parent, more specifically the mother. The souls interact during this time. The soul of the unborn child needs to communicate with the mother's soul and connect with its external energy shell, which contains information about its parents, ancestors and descendants.

When I was writing the twelfth book, I thought that life emerged in the space between the Sun and Earth, and later I realized the absurdity of this assumption. If a soul comes from other worlds, then, logically, it must originate there. Any process repeats the universal cycle, and therefore life, or that which came before life, originated simultaneously with the appearance of the universe.

I have also seen what happens to the soul of a deceased person. For three days the soul wanders around the body. During this time it is still energetically fused with it. Up until the ninth day, the soul travels between the Earth and the Sun, periodically returning to our planet. After the ninth day, the soul sheds it's outer layers and abstracts itself from earthly life. The soul begins preparing for its transition to the afterlife. It enters it after the fortieth day, somewhere between the Earth and the Sun. The forty days are needed for the disintegration of the surface layers of consciousness that connect the person to earthly life. During this time, all information collected during life needs to come together, compress and move into the subconsciousness, that is, into the subtle layers of the soul.

The soul then enters the afterlife, and stays there for about a year. If a person has not accumulated a lot of internal aggression during his life then his soul doesn't reside in the afterlife permanently, but transcends into subtler planes, into other worlds. There, the soul gains the ability to embrace more information about the universe as well as more subtle energy. The purer the soul, the closer it approaches to the Creator. In its next life such a soul can receive a unique destiny and remarkable opportunities. Souls of some particularly pure people circle around the sun up to forty days, then go into its center and travel to other worlds, bypassing the afterlife.

The soul does not appear between the Sun and the Earth, but comes out of the other worlds somewhere in this vicinity. One of its very important components comes through the center of the Sun. Generally, a person's soul remembers everything that has happened to it outside the body. Probably it is because of this that there existed the custom of burning the body of a deceased person. This was an imitation of the soul's departure through the center of the sun.

Undeveloped souls come straight from the underworld and head towards Earth. They depart just as calmly, staying away from the sun's light. Apparently, those who subconsciously remember this state try to conserve their dead body as long as possible, that is, bury it in the ground. The rites of preserving the inviolability of a deceased body, including embalmment and the erection of rich tombs and sarcophagi, carry a heightened tendency for maintaining external energetic forms. All of this powerfully binds a person's soul to the Earth and complicates his next incarnation making it more difficult for the soul to move on from the underworld to more subtle layers. Pure souls move through the center of the Sun directly into other worlds.

Suddenly, it dawns on me: it is likely that the Sun receives energy from other worlds, and the thirty three worlds which I once had a vision of are the stages of descent for Divine energy. Information gradually becomes energy, and its more subtle layers, passing into other worlds, are also transformed.

I always wondered where the future existed. If the subconsciousness, that is, the soul, reacts to the future as reality, then this future must be hidden somewhere, veiled. I later understood that the future lies in another world, another dimension, and arrives in small portions. Sometimes these portions are very large and then they may result in explosions.

Actually, this is quite logical. Our universe is constantly expanding. This means that new portions of space and time enter it. However, because time, space, and matter are inextricably linked, we must conclude that new masses of matter are constantly appearing in the universe.

New portions of time, space, and matter come from parallel worlds through the centers of the stars, making the stars spin and glow. For decades, scientists from around the world have faced an unsolvable mystery. The question appeared when it became clear that nuclear fuel would not have been sufficient to case the sun to burn. This question remains open.

The only person who approached this mystery and unveiled its secret was the Russian astronomer Kozyrev. When he was sent to a punishment cell in a Soviet concentration camp to die from cold, he internally turned to God, felt a rush of warmth, and survived. In his theory, he explained what his soul had felt at that time. The essence of his theory is that the Sun draws energy from time. His contemporaries did not understand him, and nobody continued his studies.

I keep thinking: new portions of time, arriving from other worlds, turn into energy and space. These, in turn, form the building blocks of the universe: hydrogen and helium atoms. The sun dutifully repeats the cycle of the universe's evolution and also tries to extract from itself new portions of time, space and matter. Each star has a period of youth, when it can 'get pregnant' and give birth to new planets. Then gradually the star grows old and receives less and less new portions of time. Eventually quiet old age comes, followed by death. The old star's substance will be used by other young stars.

Sometimes, however, an aging star receives a new huge portion of energy. This looks like a supernova explosion, and a new life of the same star begins. It is likely that this happens when its children, planets, do not want to or cannot become stars themselves. Planets, having emerged from the Sun, have their own personal lives and their own access to other worlds, and likewise, while evolving, turn out satellites which later become planets.

Before Kozyrev, scientists believed the Earth to be a cooling celestial body, and the Moon, respectively, to be a cold one. When Kozyrev suggested that the Moon must have some volcanic activity, he was considered insane. Later, his hypothesis was confirmed, and shocked scientists. Most likely, the Earth extracted the Moon out of itself. The Moon actively develops in the same way and receives new portions of time from parallel worlds.

If our planet gets energy and matter from the future, then it is not a cooling celestial body; on the contrary, it is an actively growing body, with the potential to become a star. It not only can, but it wants to become one. Jupiter, which has gotten new satellites, is probably already entering the intermediate stage between a planet and a star.

I am lost in thought, remembering an article about Lake Baykal. Modern technology was able to establish that its banks widen by two centimeters every year. Therefore, over the course of a million years the lake should have expanded by twenty kilometers. However, the age of

Lake Baykal is 28-30 million years, which means that its width should be not fifteen kilometers, as it is now, but six hundred. What does this fact point to? Most likely, that the process of the lake's expansion has accelerated only recently. By the way, the shores of the Red Sea are spreading too.

Lakes and seas are cracks in the earth's crust. Therefore, though it is a pity, the basic scientific hypothesis that the Earth's mass increases due to falling meteorites must be discarded. The Earth is growing from inside. This explains earthquakes, volcanic eruptions and the sliding of continental plates. Global warming is probably also connected with new, more powerful, energy. This energy arrives through the center of our planet.

Recently, I read an interesting article on the internet. In the Atlantic Ocean, not far from the islands of Bermuda, a hole in the earth's crust was discovered. Instead of crust, only a thin film separates the ocean from magma. The thickness of the earth's mantle there is very small. It was reported that a special expedition was being sent.

I wondered at how incredibly uniformed and rhythmic our universe is. This formation in the crust reminded me of the soft spot on an infant's head. While the bones in the skull are growing, there must be a place where they can form and move apart. If one such zone was found in the Atlantic, then a second zone should be located somewhere in the Pacific, according to the law of pairs and struggle of opposites.

On a subtle plane, the Sun is not a homogeneous structure. Like every living creature, it has two halves, the two poles. One part is directed towards the future; the second is directed towards the past. One part receives new energy; the other part adapts and processes it.

The Earth also consists of two halves, two poles, which are oriented differently in time. Life on Earth originated as bipolarity. Gradually, the part which was linked to the past became genetic apparatus, and the part which was oriented towards the future turned into membrane. As far as i can remember, the nervous tissue of an embryo forms from the surface epithelium. The main purpose of nerve tissue is to respond to the future, and the function of the brain of any living creature is to adapt to the future. Without predictions, we cannot control the events of the present.

So, our planet periodically receives new portions of time, energy, space and matter. I wonder what would happen if a portion of new energy were unexpectedly large? Thinking logically, the crust would break somewhere in the middle of the ocean. Plus, volcanic activity could also heighten dramatically. If magma were to flow into the depths of the ocean, it would cause the evaporation of huge quantities of the ocean's water. For some time, the entire atmosphere of the Earth would be covered with clouds; then a worldwide flood would begin. It seems that we have already been through this story.

An interesting fact: in the Bible, the flood is for some reason connected to people's sins. Over the years of my research and study of the Bible, I realized one thing: in the Bible everything is said for a reason, information of colossal importance is encrypted there. A superficial interpretation of the Bible often leads to complete nonsense. However, the correlation between natural cataclysms and the state of people living on Earth is pointed out clearly.

How can people influence portions of energy coming from other worlds? I try to trace the logical chain of thought, but a phone call interrupts my reflections. Today, I have a consultation without personal contact with my patient.

Recently, a woman admitted to me, "Before, you would to talk to me on the phone, explain everything, and give me a task. After two or three hours I would call back, you would praise me, and I would walk away feeling inspired. However, during our last session you talked to me only once and said that was enough. At first I felt this was not fair, then resentment flared up, but I quickly overcame these emotions and started working on my inner state. I've been changing for two months now. I am changing, i can feel this and know without hesitation that I have good results."

"Yes, you have changes," I said in support.

"I realized," she continued, "That my feelings of elation and joy were false. I would just relax and do nothing. So I have a request for you: do not check on us twice."

"Is this the reason that I have felt so poorly during appointments recently?" I thought to myself.

"O.K, I will try." I replied.

Now, I again hear a female voice on the phone. I ask the woman to tell me the essence of her problem.

"I have found myself in a strange situation, close to mystical," the woman says. "This is why I've come to you."

"Is it some sort of trouble or illness?" I try to determine.

She pauses and then replies, "No, not really. There was a situation that I cannot explain. However, I feel that something very serious stands behind this event. I have a feeling that I have been given a serious sign. I sense that this is a warning, and that it concerns my children."

"Tell me, in chronological order, what has happened," I ask her.

"Ok," she agrees. "More than ten years ago, i got married. My husband lives in Japan. I gave birth to two children. However, I can't permanently live and work in Japan. So I have begun living in two houses. Every year, for several months I visit my husband. I forgot to mention that my children started having problems with their health, and this prompted me to begin reading your books. In the past few years, I have studied your books seriously and have been trying to change and to learn how to love.

I've noticed that my children have also began to change for the better. Last time I visited my husband for three months, and my children and I prepared to fly back home. I had already bought tickets to Moscow. However, a day before our departure, the children had terrible earaches; moreover the inflammation, otitis, did not respond to medication. It was impossible to go home by plane so I had to return the tickets. We delayed our departure from Tokyo for two weeks. Surprisingly, in the course of a few days, the children became well again. I calmly began to pack our bags. However, a day before our departure the children's ears started hurting once again.

The story repeated itself, again we had to reschedule the date of our departure. In the past, I would have become gloomy, irritated, and would have worried about the future. In this situation, I tried to sustain the love in my soul and prayed for my children. The day of our next departure drew near and my kids felt great, but a day before departure the situation repeated itself."

"Are you in Japan now?" I ask quickly, "Are you calling from there?"

"No, I'm calling from Russia, and my kids are here with me too. Instead of three months, I stayed with my husband for half a year. When we were about to leave Tokyo, the children's ears started hurting again, but not as much and I took advantage of this. Now, for several months I have been living with a strange feeling. My children and I were given a very clear a sign from above that we must stay and live in Japan. However, I left anyway, that is, I listened to my soul and followed my feelings. Perhaps the situation was showing that my children would die in Russia, and I was given a chance to save them. I do not know. I agonize over this puzzle, and no one can help me."

"Please, list the names of the children according to their age." I ask her.

She names them, and I looked at their auras on the subtle plane. I strictly adhere to the ethics that I sense intuitively. I never look at when a person is going to die, and what will happen to him in the future. I only allow myself to see the present and then draw logical conclusions and hypotheses. The future cannot be seen in one version; this is very dangerous. I try not to see things that cannot be changed, as this brings about a feeling of helplessness and depression. I know one thing for sure: our ability to change the future is determined by the degree of our innermost change. Therefore, my main task is to help people change, and without love for God change is impossible.

So, I examine the configuration of the children's energy fields. The fields look very interesting and speak volumes. Everything becomes clear, but I want to test my assumptions.

"Please tell me the name of your husband," I ask.

She say his name, and I examined his aura with curiosity. "Does he live in Tokyo?"

"No, he lives in a small town far away from Tokyo."

"Do you want me to tell you the whole truth," I say, "Or just talk about things in general? Usually, I don't say things like this, but I feel that you are ready, so I will make an exception for you. That which you perceived as a sign telling you to stay in Japan actually meant quite the opposite. The situation was a challenge for you; you were given a serious test, and you passed it."

"What do you mean?" The patient asks with surprise.

"Please think about the kinds of emotions that the delayed departures provoked in you. They provoked the following emotions: melancholy at the collapse of your plans, frustration at your fate which did not allow you to fly, dissatisfaction with your children who got sick, because of whom your plans fell apart, regret about what had happened, irritation with your husband, who you had come to visit and who was an indirect cause of your problems. The resulting overall emotion would look like melancholy; unhappiness with yourself and your fate."

"But I did not experience these emotions," the woman says with surprise.

"This is the reason you were able to fly back to Russia," I answer calmly. "Because of this, the children's inflammation did not rise to a critical level. Please answer honestly: if you had had a strong fear before the flight, would you have stayed?"

Judging by the pause, the woman has become lost in thought. She then quickly replies, "Probably I would have stayed. However, I would have tried to overcome the fear," she adds hastily.

"This is why you were able to save your children," I say.

"Do you mean that my children will not die in Russia?" The woman asks immediately.

"They were supposed to die in Japan, but their fate changed. You were given a challenge from above to test your fear of the future. Fear arises when we focus excessively on the future and make a goal out of it. The more we become attached to the future, the more we are afraid to lose it; the more we regret that we have lost it. In a moment of danger, fear is necessary for our survival, but we must not depend on it. When we are afraid of the future, we experience a completely different fear. It is a measure of our attachment and dependence on the future. Everything that the soul is attached to it must lose, if the attachment infringes upon its love for God. So, you were supposed to lose your future together with your children and yourself. After you read my books, your soul tried to make the right choice, and the choice was made in favor of love for God.

Consciousness is a product of the future; it depends on it. If you try to control the future through your consciousness, you will not have a chance; you will fail one hundred percent. A part cannot govern the whole. Love is primary to the future, and the future depends on love. Therefore, through love for God it is possible to change the future. Your destiny slipped you a fake, focused entirely on your consciousness. You were supposed to choose between love and consciousness, and you made your choice in favor of love, in favor of emotion.

This is an interesting paradox. Feelings always give a person who is going in the direction of love and God the right hint, helping the person to survive, while the conscious mind is often only a hindrance. Feelings are much wiser than thoughts. However, if a person walks away from love and begins to worship sensual, spiritual, and physical happiness, his world paradigm changes. Then his feelings begin sending him the wrong answers, leading to illness and death.

So, consciousness cannot exist without feelings. Your usual feelings demanded that you stay, but your increasing love for God urged you to leave. Your surface feelings were associated with your attachment to life and wellbeing, stability and security, with your fear of experiencing a collapse of your desires and losing your life. However, the love in your soul won over attachment."

The woman's voice trembles and stumbles a little. "You know, I'm very anxious now, and everything is messed up in my head. I do not understand you clearly. Could you please explain this all again, more simply?"

I obediently agree. "O.K., let's start over again. In your subconscious the future became much more significant than your love for God. During your life, you reinforced this process with your emotions. You hurried, rushing into the future and worrying excessively. When your dreams and plans would collapse, you judged people who behaved unworthily, who betraying you, destroying your future. You showed signs of melancholy and disbelief in yourself, withdrawing your love from yourself and your future. However, because you began changing, you were meant to survive. Most importantly, not only you changed, but also your children. If they had not changed, it is likely that the situation would have forced them to stay with their father. You would not have been allowed to take them with you. With each delayed flight, fate was deciding whether your children would survive or not, and a lot depended on your inner state. You won, and so did your children. Now, if you decide to go with your children to live with your husband, you will have problems preventing the visit."

"Actually, that is what is going on now," admits the patient. Silence, and then she asks timidly, "Is my husband going to die?"

"Let's put it this way: your husband has little chance of survival. He is a strong idealist. Judging by his aura, he is often irritable and likes to be judgmental, especially when people let him down and behave immorally. Do you know what the Russian proverb means, 'A husband and wife are one devil?' Spouses are selected according to the law of pairs. A husband's shortcomings must be balanced by the shortcomings of his wife. Often a husband's external sins are stabilized by the internal sins of his wife. Through married life, people either help one another to overcome their own shortcomings and find love, or, losing love and friendship they sink one another."

"Tell me," asks the woman, "Can I help my husband and save his life?"

"Of course you can," I reply. "At any distance you are bound together and united on the subtle plane. Your soul can help his soul survive, but the main choice is still his. If he chooses righteousness, criticism and judgment of others over love, you will not help him. Each person has his own destiny, and it is not determined by us. We must accept this. However, this does not mean that we should give up. This means that no matter how hard we try, the last word will never be ours."

"He might become terminally ill?" the woman asks.

I think about whether or not to tell her and finally decide. "I must admit that I see this kind of picture for the first time. I always saw a possibility of death because of a person's aggressive emotions. Your husband's main danger is associated with his place of residence. There might be serious problems in the place where he is living now. I try not to look into the future and foresee the fate of countries, nations and continents. I do not know what will happen to Japan, but I can see how a particular person in a specific location may have serious problems. A person who winds up in this place is one who has no reserve of the future and whose soul has lost love to a considerable extent."

The woman asks a few more questions, and our conversation ends. "How strange," I think, " It is doubtful that I will ever see this woman again, and I have not see her before. It was just a phone consultation, a few questions and answers. Yet this conversation reveals the possible fate of other people, and maybe the future of the entire planet. "

In my mind there arises a phone conversation with a friend who left Russia fourteen years ago.

"Right now it is possible to buy very cheap airline tickets from New York to Germany," he told me, "I want to have a consultation with you in Berlin."

"I'm surprised at you," I said to him. "I have already told you everything ten times on the phone! Do you really think that during a consultation I will tell you something new?"

"You know, I am really having very big problems," he said. "Perhaps you'll find some other reason."

"At the moment I am still seeing the same thing," I said. "I see death in a few years, which is associated with your place of residence. In my opinion, you need to leave New York because you personally might have some serious problems, living there."

He kept asking me questions, and I felt like Cassandra, who no one heard. Only now, the idea of fate's inevitability dawned on me. Whatever I told him about the future, it was associated with his current inner state. He would not hear me and would not accept what I said if I was not able to help him change.

"Well, come then," I said, "To do some inner work."

Compared to Moscow, Berlin seemed very comfortable and quiet. There were no traffic jams here, and life was unhurried. Moscow at night resembles Berlin during the day. I come to Berlin mostly to rest, and consultations are a good reason to visit. The most important thing in a holiday is to change one's rhythm of life. An incorrectly selected rhythm of life can lead to an imperceptible loss of energy, and then to serious health problems.

At first I lived in Sochi and felt very well there. However, then I sensed that a new rhythm of life was necessary. I went to St. Petersburg and lived there for about five years working in construction, and then another twenty five years growing as an person.

Recently, during a lecture I was asked why such a heavy burden, the endurance of the blockade, had fallen specifically on St. Petersburg. Russia's cultural capital truly had suffered the most profound ordeals.

"Spirituality without love is a grave danger," I replied. "When money is made for the sake of money, it leads to serious problems. However, when abilities, spirituality, and consciousness lose love and focus on themselves, this is even more dangerous. Revolution is always cruelty, and it occurs because of heightened pride. In the City of Three Revolutions this tendency had always been present. The worship of spirituality and consciousness made the soul of the city ruthless, and internal aggression always transforms into external aggression. Aggression towards the outside world turns into self-destruction. It is possible that this is the reason that in the last decades of the Soviet era, the city dragged out a miserable existence.

From my point of view, the blockade was a sign from above; a sign that through suffering the citizens of Leningrad should atone for their worship of a bright future, consciousness, and spirituality. On the other hand, the fact that Leningrad survived and was not completely destroyed can also be seen as a sign: a sign that Russia will survive, as well as Russia's spirituality. So love for God and faith in Him will sooner or later return to Russia."

I walk the streets of Berlin to a place where a few people wait for me, having arrived from different cities of the world. It is a beautiful sunny day; I am in a good mood. Thoughts flow slowly, and a lot that earlier seemed a mystery is becoming clearer. "The future begins to affect the present more actively," I think. "There will be a lot of miracles soon." A miracle is an event that is not connected with the past and is inexplicable in terms of previous experience. That is, the information from the future held in it far surpasses the flow of time and information flowing from the past.

By the way, the existence of the cloning effect proves that the future is more stable in terms of information than the present. Those who set themselves the task of making a reproductive cell out of a normal one, that is, dividing DNA, where unable find a method that would cause the genetic set to split into two parts. Mechanically, it was impossible. Chemical, thermal and other influence did not work. I have no idea how scientists figured it out; perhaps, it was done by accident. They removed the DNA from a reproductive cell and put in its place the genetic apparatus of a normal cell. The membrane tore it into two parts; forced it to divide. That is, the future changed the present. Therefore, the process of cell division and the existence of life as such are not accidental or chaotic; they occur with the active intervention of the future. We can imagine that if in a living creature there arises aggression towards the future, it will simply stop multiplying.

Reflecting on this, I enter the building where the appointments are scheduled. My first patient is the friend who arrived from New York with his wife. For a while we sit in silence, collecting our thoughts. Finally, he breaks the silence with a question.

"Do you really think that New York is dying, and it is necessary to leave?"

I shake my head no. "It's impossible to know the future. This is dangerous, and I will explain why. The higher the subtle planes we enter, the cleaner our soul must be. On subtle planes time is compressed, and the future is visible. That which we call wisdom, intuition, foresight and great insight are just the ability to see the subtle planes. In the place where the entire universe compresses into a single point, there is absolute love and complete knowledge of what was, is and will be in the universe. Not only knowledge, but also control. Cognition is coming into contact with subtle planes, which automatically leads to control over them. In physics this is called the effect of the observer. If there is little love in one's soul, close contact with the higher truth and the future kills.

It is impossible to fully predict the future. Of course, a person may be given information about certain events from above, but this is another topic. Imagine that you come to a fortune-teller, and she hands you a picture of your near future. Much of what she predicted begins to come true. If she also tells you all about your past, as if she had lived it beside you, then it is really hard to doubt her prediction. Suppose her prognosis is not exact, but you took it as the absolute truth. Do you know what will happen to you then? On a subtle plane you will begin defending this paradigm, and destroying anything that doesn't fit this picture. In simple terms, you will be destroying the real future, worshiping the illusory picture of the world that you think is reality. Then," I say slowly, "You will get sick and die, because a person who has aggression towards the future simply will not receive it."

Our external physical energy comes from the past, and fine spiritual energy arrives from the future. In the Bible, there are places that many find puzzling. For example, Christ said *So I tell you, every sin and blasphemy can be forgiven- except blasphemy against the Holy Spirit, which will never be forgiven.* (Matthew 12:31). That which we call the Holy Spirit are the subtle planes where the future is hidden, where new knowledge is encrypted, containing the energy which nurtures our soul. Man is first a spiritual being, and only then a material one. The soul originated before the body, and is nourished by energy coming from the future. Christ explained this simply and clearly, *"It is written: 'Man does not live on bread alone, but on every word that comes from the mouth of God.'"* (Matthew 4:4)

The energy of the future emanates from the energy of love generated by the Creator. Distributing this energy, He decides who will stay alive and who will die. Let us recall the Old Testament: God says to Abraham, *"You will be the father of many nations."* (Genesis 17:4). This means that Abraham's soul is open for the future; it can accept a huge amount of new energy and information. Therefore, it is possible to plant the seeds of a new people and new nations in his soul.

We do not have aggression towards the future if we are not attached to it. If a person is attached to money in his soul, he will hate everyone for fear of losing his money, and then will begin to hate himself and the money which causes his suffering. After this, it will be necessary for him to lose this money, and he definitely will. Overcoming a harmful passion for money, for material hoarding, is only possible for a person who has understood and felt that there are things far more important than money, and there are pleasures greater than the feeling of coins in one's hand.

Overcoming the worship of the future is much more difficult. If the soul is nourished by energy from the future, what can be primary to the soul? The answer to this riddle has been known for two thousand years. Jesus Christ, who felt the Divine presence inside himself, often identified Himself with Love, saying, *"He that loses his life for my sake shall find it."* (Matthew 10:39) This meant that love was higher than life and the energy of the future. He for whom unity with God was more important than the future would survive, because he would not be at all aggressive towards the future. He would not depend on it.

I become lost in thought looking out the window, then once again turn to my friend. "Let's go back to Abraham. Remember how God demanded that Abraham kill his son and bring him as a sacrifice? I think that you now know what this means. It means the following: our children are our future. God put Abraham in front of a colossal dilemma. What was more important to him, love for God or love for the future? Abraham chose love for God. In this way, he overcame aggression towards the future and attachment to it, and so was able to beget new nations.

Jesus Christ talked about the same things, but in different words. What happens when a husband madly loves his wife? He can offer all sorts of reasons, but in his subconscious everything is clear: a man's love for a woman is a desire to realize his instinct of procreation; it is a hidden desire to extend himself into the future. Of course, in every human love there is Divine love, but this is the part we often forget about. When a man madly loves his children, this means that he loves himself in them, his future. Christ said, *"A man's foes shall be they of his own household,"* (Matthew 10:36). This meant that love for God may be obscured by love of one's loved ones, one's children and ultimately the future."

My companion is lost in thought for a while. "So if one is excessively attached to one's wife and children, one may lose his future."

I nod in satisfaction. "Exactly so. I see you are beginning to understand me. And when we strengthen this attachment through jealousy, judgment, and melancholy, we may lose the future even faster. Why is being resentful, judgmental and melancholic dangerous? Because these are forms of rejecting love. All that makes us reject God must be lost. You know, the Chinese have an old saying, "If you want to take revenge on someone, dig two graves simultaneously." The laws by which the soul lives are equally just for the believer and the atheist."

My companion smiles, remembering something, and interrupts me. "Okay, now let's imagine that a fortune teller predicts my future more or less accurately. This is help for me. What is wrong with it?"

I shrug my shoulders. "Do you know how to determine if a person is attached to something or not? Well, the first indicator is clear: a person cannot bear the loss of that to which he is attached. Before the loss of the object of his attachment, the person worships it, and after the loss, the person hates others or himself for losing it. Worship and hatred always walk in pairs; one is inextricably linked to the other."

I smile, looking at him. "It is possible to worship God without attachment arising because God is eternal, and it is impossible to lose Him. Therefore love for God can never give rise to aggression. Eternity in our hearts does not require protection. So, if a fortune teller tells you something very nice, you will begin to internally worship this future in your soul and you will lose it. If the predicted events are very unpleasant, you may experience fear and despair. In this way you may also damage your future and lose it."

"What about Assol, who dreamed of scarlet sails and a beautiful captain? After all, her dream came true."

"Sometimes our dreams are a reflection of what will happen to us. If you want something, then it is already possible. If you do not worship your dreams, do not panic or fall into despair because of your fear of losing them, do not experience resentment and hatred towards those who interfere with your dreams, then the dreams can come true."

Once again my friend lost himself in thought, looking straight ahead. "Is it for this reason, that in the Old Testament it says a fortuneteller and astrologer shall burn? Does this mean that knowledge of the future is always a bad thing?"

I shake my head no. "If knowledge of the future pushes you towards love and forces you to care for your soul, it can be helpful. If the knowledge causes fear, melancholy, or excessive joy, it is harmful. Therefore, prophets spoke about the future not of individuals but of entire nations. That knowledge of the future helped humanity survive. People turned to the prophets in order to save their souls, and to fortunetellers to save their bodies and wallets."

There is a slight pause, and then he asks again, "So will New York perish or not?"

I shrug again. "I cannot see into the future, it is dangerous for me; moreover, I am useless as a predictor. However, you personally will have serious problems living in New York."

"All right," he says suddenly, "Let's suppose that I am excessively attached to my family, and because of this my future closes. If we move to a different place I will need to survive, to adapt to a new job, and I will not have time for my family. My soul will balance out, and my future will open up. Is this option possible?"

I shrug. "Of course! The future has many versions. By the way, do you know what a man who will soon lose his future looks like?"

He glances at me with interest. "Do you want to give me a recipe?"

I nod. "I am now going to reveal this terrible secret to you. If you have several options for future development, you will not become attached to them because it is impossible to pursue multiple targets simultaneously. If you feel that God controls the future, then you will be forced to assume that there are unknown options for what will happen to you. However, if you forget about God and have only one model of the future, you're doomed to worship this model more and more, and your fear, hatred and melancholy will intensify.

A person who has partially lost his future first experiences troubles, then quarrels and resentments, and then diseases. If his reserve of the future is almost exhausted, then there are serious misfortunes, destruction of family, incurable or fatal diseases. If a group of people worship the future, as it was with the Communists, its aggression becomes noticeable and can kill millions and tens of millions of people. Then, in the best case, a loss of future will result in the death and decay of the government."

He quickly glances at me. "Are you saying that America is 'fixated' on the future?"

I laugh. "In any case, the U.S. government asserts this. America worships its security and superiority. A sense of entitlement and supremacy over other nations indicates a poor state of affairs. This was the attitude of the Jewish people before the Jewish War and the full destruction of Jerusalem. Those who staged the October Revolution in Russia had this same feeling. Many Bolsheviks were absolutely sure of their righteousness and the impeccability of the model they had created for the future. First, they began exterminating their own people, and later were destroyed themselves. The meat grinder known as the 'path to communism,' worked tirelessly for many decades."

My companion, frowning, looks at me. "But what can happen to New York? An explosion again?"

I look in front of me, putting my hands together, palms down. "Imagine that the earth's crust moves apart in different directions," I say, parting my hands. "The vacant cavity that appears is rapidly filled with ocean water. Then a mound of water is formed. The water first rushes from the shore for tens of kilometers, and then quickly rushes back. Something similar has already happened in Thailand." I look at him and continue, "Of course, there arrises a reasonable question: even if energy does arrive from the future, why must it arrive in such large quantities? After all, Lake Baykal and the Red Sea are only gradually expanding."

For a moment I ponder, and then say, "When I read the Old Testament, I noticed that cataclysms and the state of human society are closely linked to each other. I used to think that this was mere intimidation, but then I realized that nothing in the Bible is without reason. That which we might think of as intimidation or punishment is in fact encrypted universal law. Because of this, I arrived at a curious hypothesis. Imagine that life in its physical aspect originated on the Earth and is an essential part of it. On a higher plane, our universe and everything in it is united. Therefore, people living on Earth can affect the future of the planet with their energy. Now imagine that there is a group of people with strong internal aggression towards the future, and their state is transmitted to the entire planet. What will happen to a planet that shows aggression towards the future? It, like any organism, can get sick and die.

We will not focus on death at the present moment, but instead will talk about sickness in detail. Imagine that the energy of the future comes from other worlds as time, space, and matter. To be more precise, time arrives in the form of energy, space and matter. If the planet is aggressive towards the future, it hides from it, as if building up a dam. The energy accumulates, and sooner or later, the dam bursts. A large package of energy can lead to cataclysms on the planet.

A person gets sick and dies if he has a shortage of the future. A depleted future is a loss of energy. However, a person can also get sick and die from an excess of future, because he will not be able to adapt a large portion of energy.

So, a person first sins with his body; his behavior. Gradually this becomes a habit, registering in his consciousness, then in his paradigm, as it happened in Sodom and Gomorrah. That which exists constantly with stability in a person's conscious mind passes into his subconscious, that is, into his soul, and begins to be in contact with the future. Aggression at the level of the body is not dangerous for the future and for subtle planes. However, when aggression goes into the subconscious it has a completely different effect. If people worship material and sensual happiness, they hurt their soul, and therefore their future. If people worship spirituality and the highest sensual aspects they become inwardly aggressive in the same way. Any worship that distances a person from the Creator makes a person's soul aggressive and deprives them of the future.

If you look at modern civilization critically, it is easy to see that the notion of belief in God has become a formality. Science has won over religion, forcing people to worship the body and instincts. At best, this worship shifts from the present into the future, as it was with the Communists. At the present time, we can speak about the aggression of our entire civilization. Naturally, the leading countries are the most aggressive. These are the countries that have made a breakthrough in civilization at the expense of the soul; the future. These are the United States of America, Japan, and China."

I become lost in thought, turning to the window. "However, there is one curious piece of information. Often when a child might die his parents act as a safety net, getting sick and dying in their stead. The parent of Western civilization, which has now engulfed almost the entire world, can be considered to be Israel. Therefore, Israel might have serious problems in the upcoming years.

I smile. "There is also another ancestor, southern Africa. According to my diagnosis, it turns out that life in its physical form originated in the Indian Ocean and emerged from the water onto land in southern Africa. Therefore, future cataclysms are also possible in this area."

My friend supports me. "They say that 2012 is the year when serious cataclysms will begin, and in 2015 an entire continent might vanish."

"I do not want to look into the future," I say. "I know one important thing: our innermost state is linked to the future and influences it. If we take care of our soul more than our body, then instead of decay and self-destruction, growth and creation will come to us."

Chapter 3

The Airplane

The flight from Moscow to Singapore lasts nine hours. This time can be either painful or joyful. It depends on our attitude. In a newspaper information appeared about people sometimes dying after flights that last for longer than eight hours. Therefore, it is now recommended that passengers move around a little after every two hours sitting still in a chair.

Why is inertia so dangerous? It is possible to explain this logically: if a person has flawed blood vessels and thick blood, there might be stagnant processes in the body, which are intensified by an inconvenient posture. However, perhaps this is not the main reason. Often in the morning after a good night's sleep, a person looks in the mirror and cannot recognize himself. His face is swollen; wrinkles have deepened. It seems that aging occurs during sleep. Of course, it is possible to make one's condition worse by drinking a lot of water and eating heartily before going to bed. Still, some people eat practically once a day, mainly in the evening, and wake up in the morning feeling energetic and rested. Therefore, the reason for this lies not so much in food, but more in emotions. Emotions are energy.

I look out of the window, into the boundless sky. The sun will rise soon; the sky is becoming light blue, with clouds a pearly pink color. I recall a saying from Lao Tzu, "All beneath Heaven, the weak and the tender overcome the sturdy and the strong." When we are born, we are weak and vulnerable. When we die, we are stiff and hardy. Divine love comes to the universe as a primary impulse. This primary impulse splits into two currents of time, and energy appears. This energy is then arranged into space and matter.

Weakness and vulnerability are the states in which high energy has not yet been converted into form. Gradually, energy is spent and weakens, while form strengthens and evolves. When the content is almost entirely depleted, the form is maximally strong and reaches its zenith, but already contains no energy. Its further development is death and decay. The more energy of love lies at the heart of any process, the more opportunities its form has for development.

I often explained to my patients the importance of the first impulse in starting a new project or company. If you conceive or plan something with a feeling of envy and resentment, or desire to do it only for money, the enterprise is doomed to failure and collapse. A rotten seed will never produce a healthy sprout. If, on the other hand, you're looking for an opportunity to bring some excess energy to fulfillment, to realize yourself, to enhance the feeling of flight that accompanies busy creative work, then the project will go well.

Long ago it was noticed that children going into big sports and dreaming to make lots of money started experiencing strange things; regardless of effort, talent, and financial backing, traumas and setbacks began happening. Unexplainable as it was, it seemed that fate itself did not favor such children and did not allow them to achieve something in life.

I remember how I explained this to one hockey player, "The only wishes that come true are those that won't make you their slave. You want to score a goal so intensely that you begin to be entirely dependent on this desire. When the soul begins to depend on something, love disappears and aggression comes. The love of a attached and dependent person turns into passion and begins hurting the person as well as the one he loves. Passion, unlike love, is always aggressive. This is because passion is desire that has won over love. In passion, the desire to receive is invariably stronger than the desire to give. Therefore, it is basically a predatory feeling. A bandit desires to gain as much as possible and give as little as possible. A person seized by passion resembles this same bandit, rejecting the Divine. One should always internally detach oneself from desires so as not to become their slave. Without love, this detachment is impossible."

"Imagine," I said to the athlete, "That you attack the net while your soul is full of subconscious aggression. Scoring a goal is a reward. The flash of joy that occurs at this time penetrates your subconscious and reinforces your behavior. Try learning a foreign language in a state of joy and in the state of frustration. In a joyful state, you will be able to learn the basics in several days. On the other hand, in a state of fear, uncertainty, melancholy or displeasure, you will not be able to learn the fundamentals of the language for years."

I often consulted immigrants who for many years were unable to learn the language of their new country, although they tried very hard. The reason is very simple and is concealed in human emotions. Joy is the code of access to the subconscious, and whatever enters the subconscious stays there. The subconscious remembers everything. If a child is not taught how to rejoice in the right way, later he may become an invalid.

When a child watches scenes of violence on television in a state of joy, as well as various sexual scenes, and hears constant calls to enrichment at all costs, in his subconscious this information links with positive emotions. Later, in order to bring about a feeling of joy, he will need to kill, rape, or marvel at a huge amount of money in his bank account.

One serial killer told an investigator how he had embarked on this path. One day he was watching a television film which showed the murder of a woman. Suddenly, at this moment, he experienced an orgasm. After this he could experience orgasm only when he was killing and raping his victims.

From ancient times, society has instructed children on when they should rejoice and when they should not. This was called moral upbringing and was always connected with religion. Now, religion and morality have been separated from state affairs. Instead, science has begun to explain what we should be happy about. It proceeds on the premise that a human being is only the physical body; the concept of the soul is a myth for science. When morality is bound only to the needs of the body, a natural process of worship of the body, subjugation to the desires of the body, happens. Naturally, this return to paganism is accompanied by the disintegration of society.

Once again my thoughts return to the athlete i had consulted. "You attack the net with intense aggression," I told him. "Externally, you are a sportsman who wants to score a goal by any means necessary. Internally you are a bandit, willing to kill anyone in order to win. However, your children will inherit not your form but your content. The point of development is that a new form negates the previous one. However, its essence, its content, is preserved and continues its development. Therefore, your children will be murderers and robbers. If this process penetrates the subconscious and beyond, your children will simply be sick, paralyzed and die. In order for them to survive, you must not score goals and reinforce your aggressive state."

The athlete looked discouraged. "How should I pray in order to not be aggressive?" He asked, confused.

"For you, love has become synonymous with kindness, in other words with gentleness, care, and tenderness. However, God not only gives, but also takes away. The same can be said about love. If you love your child, you are obligated to teach him to overcome pain. For this, you must put him in difficult circumstances, or else he will definitely have various problems. So, learn to be not only soft but also firm, while preserving love."

"Are there any exercises to practice this?" he asked with curiosity.

"To start, you can just hang up a bag, and hit it with your fists while maintaining a smile. As soon as you feel tension and lose the smile, you must immediately stop the process. Also, you and I will try the following: take rackets and go play tennis. The feeling of love is usually accompanied by a feeling of flight, joy and happiness. For this reason, try not to lose this feeling of lightness and joy in your soul, especially at the moment you are hitting the ball."

I became lost in thought, looking at him, and then continued. "If you learn to do this, you will achieve great success, and will develop greater abilities. This is just the first step. However, at this stage your energy level will be much higher than the current level, and a dangerous substitution might take place undetected. Your feeling of excitement and joy can imperceptibly obstruct your feeling of love. In this condition it is possible to break the jaws of others while feeling joy. In this case, your aggression will go deeper into the subconscious and will harm your descendants even more. What is the way out of this dangerous situation? The answer is the following. The higher one's level of energy, the more effort one should exert in order to preserve the feeling of love. Love allows us to feel another person as ourselves. Then harsh actions toward another person will teach them, that is, facilitate change. If you do not know how to love, any harsh actions will always be destructive, not educational. What is resentment, the desire for revenge, the desire to punish another? They are attempts to destroy one's offender. Translated into the language of philosophy, it is the desire to destroy a conflict and its cause. Absolute lack of conflict is lack of development and death."

I recall another story. It was told to me by a wrestler. "I was unbeatable," he said. "I knew my capabilities, my strength, and my technical expertise. Internally, I was ready to tear apart any opponent and felt that my will was the most powerful. However, weird things happened to me during matches, unavoidable injuries and setbacks, and I could never get to the finals. However, calm, good-natured guys got to the finals and won."

So, desire should not blind a person. In this case, it is natural to ask: in which case does desire blind? As a rule, when a person focuses on the desire and forgets about everything else; about love, kindness, morality. In other words, it is good and healthy to have desires, but the strength of the desire must not exceed one's feeling of love. Therefore, one person can have various desires which will be beneficial to him, while another person will have the same desires and will become hostile, then get seriously ill and die.

The energy of desire is a form of wealth, just the same as money, a car, a summer house, or an apartment. Just as with any wealth, desire can be dangerous if a person is not ready for his own happiness.

The athlete was lost in thought, and I saw that some points were not clear to him.

"You say that harsh actions must be educational measures, but what kind of education can there be when people beat each other up on the ice? It is no secret that there are some hockey players who score goals, and some who make money by punching faces. So how am I supposed to maintain inner detachment?" he asked.

"Everything depends on how you distribute your energy," I answered. "Imagine a master of martial arts, a person who for many years practiced a science that taught him how to kill. However, eventually he realized that the purpose of martial arts is not to kill an opponent, because anyone who has his own opinion is already an opponent. If any conflict is resolved by eliminating the opposing side, sooner or later you will want to kill the entire universe and yourself along with it. The master then made a discovery: one should not kill an opponent, but rather suppress him, show him one's superiority, and in order to maintain this superiority one must establish contact with the opponent to understand him better.

Time goes by, and the master makes an even greater discovery. It turns out that in order to win, it is necessary not so much to overpower your opponent as to control him. At the highest level, an opponent is not even aware that he is being controlled. But for this you must know and feel the person you are controlling very well. 'This is the pinnacle of martial arts,' realized the master, 'true victory comes without a physical battle. Real martial arts is the ability to control other people, working on a level which they are not even aware of. Real control happens through the future. The greater your ability to handle the future, the more subtly and inevitably you can control others.' At some point, the master has a sudden revelation. In order to control others, you need to learn how to control yourself. A greedy, envious, resentful man will always be dependent, and therefore will be unable to control others. Only by truly changing ourselves are we able to change the future and control other people. In order to overcome ourselves, that is, our instincts, body and consciousness, we need to gain another foothold. In order to feel free from our animal and human nature, we need to acknowledge our own divine nature, to sense that this is the only eternal reality. In this way, it turns out that the only real purpose of martial arts is to feel God inside oneself. Even when athletes batter each other, energy distributes across all levels simultaneously. If one's main vector shifts to a desire to destroy one's opponent, there will be injuries, illnesses and mishaps. If the vector moves towards self-development, then there will be fewer injuries and misfortunes. Sooner or later the universe needs to return to the Creator; for this the level of love in our hearts must constantly increase. Someone who loses love must die; someone who increases love will evolve."

I look out of the window again, and watch the expanding sunrise. In the East, people meditate sitting still for hours and feel fine. Meanwhile, a westerner sits still for a few hours and gets sick. I have never come across attempts to explain this phenomenon, though the explanation is fairly simple if we turn to the concept of energy.

When scientists measured the rhythm of a meditating man's brain, they saw an interesting picture. First, all rhythms demonstrated the onset of sleep. The meditator was actually calmly sleeping. However, suddenly there was an activation of certain areas in the brain. Brain activity followed, indicating that the man was alert in his dream. A western person is accustomed to giving energy through interaction with the outside world. If a person is motionless for a long time, his level of energy drops significantly, his metabolism slows down, and pathological processes may begin.

If a person sits in stillness and begins to meditate or pray, his energy levels remain high, and inertia ceases to be dangerous. So, energy is at the root here. Incidentally, the same thing happens in sleep. If a person goes to bed in a gloomy mood, weighed down by a ton of problems, his energy field drops twofold while he sleeps and consequently the process of aging accelerates. A person's lowest energy level is at four o'clock in the morning. For this reason, the soundest sleep takes place at this time. Doctors have long since noticed that patients usually die at daybreak.

Why do we say three o'clock at night, but four o'clock in the morning? Because morning indicates a rise in energy, and begins at four o'clock. The finest and purest energy comes between four and seven o'clock in the morning. For this reason, it is best to pray during these early morning hours. Not for naught do we have the saying, "God gives to those who get up early" (or "The early bird catches the worm.")

A desire that appears in the morning has a much greater chance of being fulfilled. However, if the desire is wrong, its fulfillment is dangerous. For this reason, passionate, jealous and dependent people must oversleep the time of desire's fulfillment. Instead of larks they become owls and usually wake up at eleven or twelve o'clock in the morning when the internal energy of desire is greatly weakened. After four p.m. energy begins to slowly decline, and after eight pm this drop in energy accelerates. For this reason perhaps, harmonious people should wake up at four or five a.m. and go to sleep around nine p.m. This schedule weakens their external energy but enhances their subtle energy. Then, a person's energy is allocated to strategic needs more than immediate necessities.

It turns out that 'larks' are more inclined to store energy, while 'owls' often use and realize it. "This is an interesting topic," I think, "I will need to return to it." In the morning, it is true that desires are more likely to be fulfilled. However, in order for them to not be harmful, their 'roots' must be pure. Therefore, it's better to pray before desiring. This clarifies why in the old days any true believer started his early morning with a prayer.

"How interestingly and magnificently life is organized," I think, "Everything is woven from opposites. If you want to build a house with high walls, first you have to take care of other things; specifically, you must construct the foundation. The more intensely you long for the fulfillment of a desire, the more you must detach yourself from it, forget about it and concentrate on its foundation: the feeling of love. Walls grow out of a foundation; desires grow out of love. Those who build walls on sand will quickly get a sense of happiness, but then this same happiness will bury them.

Science, worshiping the physical body, calls for the immediate fulfillment of desires. Religion encourages the renunciation of desires. Each party believes that truth is on its side. In fact, both parties are right, and at the same time both are wrong. To build walls without a foundation is madness, but it is silly not to build walls when the foundation has already been built. Only the feeling of love can decide what and when should be built.

Why does religion always give birth to science? Because religion is the foundation. Comprehension of the world began in a state of detachment from it. Helping people to detach themselves from this world and from the worship of it, the world's religions filled people's originating desires with a high level of energy.

Modern civilization has built high walls, and it's foundation, created a long time ago, is already cracking under the weight of these walls. A smart owner won't wait until the walls tumble down. He will immediately halt construction, and work on securing the foundation. However, many begin thinking about the foundation only when the walls have already collapsed.

I look again at the bottomless blue sky. The plane is preparing to land. The world I left behind will soon give way to a new one. In this new world, I too will become a little different, and therefore will be able to detach myself from some of my problems, and communicate with my true self.

Chapter 4

Singapore

I have gotten used to waking up early. During two morning hours it is possible to do more than during an eight hour day. I wake up and look out the hotel window. The early sunrise pours in through the gaps between the window curtains. The hotel is situated near the embankment of the river which flows through this city. An hour long walk in the morning, when the city is still asleep, is a great pleasure. Singapore is immersed in quietness. Birds sing. I go along the waterfront, gazing at the small houses and skyscrapers in the distance. Yesterday there was a city tour.

Before, this city island was a British colony. After the British left, the local population lacked a program for further development. How were they going to continue their existence? This was the main question of the time. The residents of Singapore appealed to the United Nations, asking for experts to be sent. One of the best professionals asked to design the city's program set forth two conditions. The first condition was for the government of Singapore not to include communists, and the second condition was for there to be no revenge on the British, and no dismantling of the monuments which they had put up. After all, it would be in a large part the former colonists who would invest in the development of Singapore.

These recommendations were related to economic strategy. However, it turns out that they had a very close relevance to psychology and bio-energetics. The new state was built not on principles of revenge, and not on the desire to seize from a few and divide among many.

Actually, the concept was very simple: not to regret the past, and not to look for scapegoats; to respect the smart and energetic, support the poor, ensure equal conditions for children and students. Officials were paid well. At the same time, strict laws prohibiting stealing were passed.

Seventy percent of the local population does not currently pay taxes. If a family's income is less than a certain sum, it is considered unethical to take more away from them. The nation is flourishing. Singapore's feedback mechanism works perfectly; an unjust law or event gets immediate public assessment, followed by proper adjustment.

The current moral paralysis in Russia is largely a result of socialist thinking. The absolute infallibility of the ideas of Socialism automatically transferred onto its party; the party and its leaders were also considered sinless. For this reason, even their most obtuse actions were not subject to public assessment and critique.

When feedback is missing from a way of thinking it becomes flat and static. Then, any plan or model of the future is seen through rose colored glasses. Feedback is pain, misfortune, and trouble. What is an illness? It is God's feedback to a human being. Incorrect behavior gives rise to illness. A person realizes his imperfections and this pushes him towards personal development and a fuller comprehension of the world.

Anyone who thinks about the future, imagining both potential minuses and pluses, adds the pain of possible loss to the sweetest of his dreams of the future. The more possible negative factors a person can modulate, the more likely it is that his dreams will come true. As always, there are two potential extremes in this type of thinking.

When a person is driving on a dangerous road, any prohibiting or warning sign is an encrypted notification of danger, even death. A normal person will retain the desire to go ahead, but at the same time will closely monitor perilous signs. The signs will help him to foresee possible danger and to avoid it. That is, a normal person's consciousness can accommodate opposites.

People with underdeveloped psyches will fall into extremes. One will think in this way, "Psychologists say that you shouldn't imagine negative things or else these things will happen to you. Therefore, I will not look at these negative signs. I am in a good mood, so why should I ruin it?" Another will sink into depression: "There are many unpleasant signs, and the road is so dangerous; I better not go anywhere."

The Russian aphorism, "We wanted the best, but everything turned out as usual," would probably be difficult to understand in Singapore. In Russia, a person can concentrate on pleasure, on a bright future, and chase away any unpleasant thoughts, of course never achieving this happiness. The more happiness we get, the more pain we'll endure at its loss, and those who aren't ready for the pain will not obtain the happiness.

A highly developed civilization implies a high level of responsibility. If a mountain climber wants to conquer the highest peak, that is make an extremely complex technical passage, he must have the highest level of external and internal training or else the he will die.

In Russia during the last fifteen years there was an attempt to build a highly advanced society, with no responsibility. External responsibility is thought through laws. Internal responsibility is a high level of moral development in each person. Today Russian society is feverishly trying to storm the top of the mountain. However, this 'alpinist' has virtually no equipment. He is poorly prepared physically, and morally weak; that is, he is ready to betray and push away a comrade for the sake of his own survival. Alpinists of this level will not last long as a team. Each member, instead of helping one other, will push each another into the abyss. Therefore, despite the present oil wealth there is a growing tendency of disintegration in Russia.

Not a single immoral civilization or government has lasted for very long. Morality not only helps us to preserve love and belief in God, but also helps us to feel united with other people. It helps us not to kill, rob and envy our fellow men. Morality tells us: do not rob yourself, do not use up the stores that you have saved for winter. An immoral person cannot think strategically. A greedy person cannot be wise. For this reason, immoral people can propose brilliant projects for the present time, without understanding that these projects will become suicidal tomorrow or the day after.

I am distracted from these thoughts when a bird suddenly flies past me. It looks like a black thrush. The bird lands near me on the stone slabs of the embankment. Then it flies over to a small bronze sculpture representing a boy with a dog. The sculpture looks very nice: it is an ordinary boy with a dog snuggled up against him. However, there was something unusual. I examine the sculpture closely, and suddenly it dawns on me: the boy has a Chinese face!

In Singapore, two thirds of the population is of Chinese origin. "It is unusual for me now to see a sculpture of a boy with slanted Chinese eyes," I think. "However, in thirty or forty years, half of all children born in Russia will have these eyes." I enter an underground passage, built below a bridge crossing the river. A sign on the wall reads that the fine for riding a bicycle in the passage is $1000. Chewing gum is not sold in Singapore at all, and for an abandoned cigarette butt one can pay a $500 fine. The law helps to control animal desires and forces people to care about the interests of others. Moreover, not only physical interests, but also spiritual ones. "Civility and responsibility," I keep thinking, "perfectly complement each other here."

A beggar sits in the middle of the underground passageway; he is poorly dressed, with a plastic cup for alms. In two days, I came across only one beggar. He sees me and shakes the cup, waiting for charity. I search my pockets, but find no change there. I part my hands, "Sorry, brother, you are out of luck today." He nods in understanding and sets the cup aside. "Why is this man a beggar?" I wonder.

I look at his aura, and everything becomes clear. He is completely unable to hold a punch when it comes to his destiny; his soul desires wellbeing, happiness, and stability too much. If he were to acquire such happiness, he would most likely become ill and die. The worse a person lives, the less unhappy he is about his fate. There is simply nothing to rely on except the soul's love, which no one can ever take away. Only we ourselves can turn away from love.

This person's energy field is shrinking, that is to say, he has practically no energy left. However, in absolute poverty he is likely to survive, and will probably remain healthy. I instinctively fumble in my breast pocket and unexpectedly find a five dollar bill. Remembering that today is the beginning of the New Year according to the Oriental calendar, I return and hand the beggar five dollars. "Happy New Year!" I say. He smiles and thanks me. Suddenly, something unexpected happens. His aura changes; there was no death in it any more.

I continue my walk and at the same time I try to figure out what has happened. Is it possible that joy can change a man in such a way? I remember an article that described a poor woman in Russia who won about a million dollars. A year later she was found in her familiar company of homeless people. It is not a question of money, but of the feeling of happiness which a person must know how to sustain. The Money is not primary. If there is no harmony in the soul, money goes away.

Scientists conducted a study which revealed that joy and positive emotions enhance the immune system. Conversely, if troubles overshadow the feelings of love and joy inside a person, his immune system weakens and various diseases develop. At present, doctors are trying to methodically examine disease as a concept, and have come to the undeniable conclusion that it is useless treating individual organs or diseases if the immune system is depleted. To do this, it is necessary to understand what the immune system is.

With time scientists will come to the conclusion that the immune system is energy. This energy is somewhat unusual in nature; it is not like muscular, physical energy. Our emotions and feelings are also energy. A maximum amount of energy exists between two opposite potentials. The highest potential is the difference between currents of time.

The Buddha said, "Only here and now." Christ said, *"So do not worry about tomorrow; for tomorrow will care for itself. Each day has enough trouble of its own."* (Matthew 6:34). It turns out that those who tend to live in tomorrow, internally shifting themselves there, fixate on one potential and their energy drops. Those who live in memories of the past will likewise lose energy, and with it their immune system. Therefore, if you want to determine whether a disease is creeping up on you or not, look at yourself from a distance. Determine where your main feeling of happiness is located. If it is in the past then you are already sick and have no energy. If it is in the future, you will experience an even greater loss of energy and face serious health problems. Only if your greatest happiness is in the present will you will be healthy.

Sometimes it is hard to determine where one's main positive emotion is located. Here is a hint: if you have regrets about the past or can't accept what has happened then your main happiness is in the past and you will constantly lose your energy through regret. If you have excessive worries about the future, or fixation on the future, fear, and melancholy, then you no longer live in the present and will continue losing energy through melancholy. On the subtle plane there is no pronounced past and future. There, everything exists in the present. For this reason, excessive focus on the past or the future is actually aggression towards time and the destruction of its structure.

Sometimes I would allow myself to see a person's future, and perceived it as the past. In our consciousness, which is associated with the physical form, we first see an empty plot and then a finished house. We say that there had been no house in the past, and that it exists now, in the present. On the subtle plane, the house existed before its creation and will continue to exist after its destruction. So, information about an object is present before its manifestation and after its disappearance.

Our subconscious is linked to subtle planes, where the course of time is completely different. There, the past, present, and future are visible simultaneously, and that which will happen often looks as though it has already occurred. The subtler the plane we come to, the greater coverage of past and future we observe. Energy turns into information. The universe is absolutely united on the subtlest planes. For this reason, immersing our desires into our subconscious we begin to control the surrounding world.

Joy is the password for access into the subconscious. What remains is to figure out what the feeling of joy is. For example, why do we rejoice when we receive a gift? Why do we rejoice when we move out of a tiny room into a spacious apartment? Why do we rejoice when we receive a lot of money? And why does joy soon disappear, and we become used to the happiness we have received?

Through comparison and analysis, I came to the following conclusion. The feeling of joy in people is associated with a release of energy. The subtler the level of energy, the more beautiful the feeling of joy we experience. The highest feeling of happiness a human being can experience is love for God. Through this feeling we receive higher energy, and with it we experience love towards our close ones and the surrounding world.

The universe is constantly expanding. This means that love and joy are always coming into it, and each instant this energy supports the existence of everything in the universe. If a living or non-living being breaks the universal laws, it loses the energy of love and joy and quickly dies. Thus, the law for survival and evolution in our universe is the preservation and multiplication of love. It was probably for this reason that one of the Apostles said, *"Rejoice in the Lord always,"* (Philippians 4:4) meaning that love and joy are closely interrelated.

When I tried to learn foreign languages, I noticed an interesting characteristic. In a shop, taxi or street I easily remembered any phrases. On the other hand, at home, I slowly tried to memorize the language and the results were much worse. I later understood that the secret lay in what was happening outdoors. In a shop you move around, do things, communicate. At home, you sit, expending a minimum amount of energy. For this reason, if you walk around the room while memorizing words the result will be much better.

Why is it that during youth we have a better memory and find it easier to learn languages ? Because we give more energy when we are young. Often old people joke, "My memory is cheating on me with dementia." This is simply a severe drop in subtle energy. It has been noticed that creative people retain a fine memory until their old age. This is explained by their training, but actually it is because a high level of energy has been maintained. It is because of this that creative people age more slowly.

Recently, I read an interesting newspaper article. Doctors had devised a program to improve patients' memories. Unexpectedly, they noticed an unusual link: with improved memory, a male's sexual potency improved as well. That is, the subtle energy which supports sexual potency is also essential for memory retention.

Having read these lines, a person may decide that they have discovered the secret of happiness and health. You just need to smile and feel joy more often, and as a result you will be healthy and wealthy. However, there is a little secret. Ask yourself, "Where will I get energy to be constantly happy and smiling?" The answer to this question is simple: you get this energy from the feeling of love.

It turns out that if there is no feelings of love in the soul, yet a person still smiles and feels happy, then it is possible for him to deplete his subtle planes, that is, drain energy from his descendants, steal it from his destiny and future, that is, destroy strategic reserves for the sake of a short-term comfortable life.

So, love always turns into joy, but joy cannot always become love. Naturally, one wishes to ask: "How do I learn to love?" These days, I am asked this question more and more frequently. The answer is so simple and familiar that it's hard to believe.

To start, try doing the most basic thing: abide by the Ten Commandments given to mankind three and a half thousand years ago. The first thing that must be understood is that the highest happiness possible is unity with God. If the soul does not accept this, it will inevitably switch to something else and will lose subtle energy. Therefore, one must only worship One God. In order to feel the Divine inside oneself as reality, one must periodically become detached from all earthly affairs. Such a day may be Friday, Saturday or Sunday; also, once a year detachment may last for about one and a half months.

When a person has a lot of love in his soul, he must constantly spend energy in a form of creativity, care, work. If a person steals, plunders, kills, or worships external pleasures, he switches into the mode of consumption and loses love. Sex without love is aimed at receiving pure pleasure. Energy is spent not for the sake of developing the feeling of love, and not for the sake of bringing children into the world, but for pleasure for its own sake. Thus, promiscuity also deprives a person of love.

In order to preserve love, it is necessary to periodically undergo inner cleansing through pain. Subconsciously, we always love our parents, who gave us life. Therefore, respect towards our parents, forgiveness, and the removal of any grievances felt towards them helps us experience pure and selfless love. A dependent person is always a consumer, wanting to receive much more than he gives. Naturally, he will not learn to love until he overcomes this state.

Humankind has known the Ten Commandments for three and a half thousand years. It would be interesting to find out if at least one percent of all people observe them? Joy is the access code to the subconscious. Love, respectively, is an even greater opportunity to penetrate into the subconscious. So, when a person falls in love he must ideally satisfy the laws of the universe, or he will die. Therefore, for a greedy, dependent, righteous, superior and indulgent person, who worships his desires and instincts, love becomes a fatally dangerous feeling. This means that in the face of love, one needs to be absolutely vulnerable, both spiritually and physically. One must be sincere in the presence of love. One must be willing to sacrifice, caring and generous before love. In the face of love one must also be tough, so as not to worship desires and instincts. It is necessary to prepare in advance for the feeling of love, because our paradigm forms our reflexes over the course of years. It is with reflexes that we respond to the feeling of love.

It turns out that our first flash of the feeling of love, like a tuning fork, checks to see if we are in harmony with the universal laws. A person who fears this feeling and runs from it actually destroys the feedback mechanism that connects his soul to the universe. *"And because lawlessness will be increased, the love of many will grow cold."* (Matthew 24:12) said Christ about two thousand years ago. Now we are seeing where this process can lead.

For several hundred years, mankind has been storming the subconsciousness. Hypnotists, psychologists, doctors, individuals in the secret services have been trying to do this. Of course it would then be possible to cure any diseases, develop any abilities, gain power over the world! However, on a subtle level, power over the world is power over God, and representatives of this trend sooner or later subject their entire lineage to extinction; destroy their own descendants.

Twenty years ago I read a typewritten text describing the development of higher abilities. The student volunteers who were experimented on were tightly swaddled and remained in this state for a few days. The energy normally used for communication and physical movement was redirected from the external world towards their internal world.

The students could smell soap brought into an adjacent room. With a little concentration, they began seeing things that happened behind the separating wall. I think this phenomenon can be easily explained.

Any event first occurs on a subtle level and only then is duplicated on the external level. On subtle planes there are no walls, and there is no difference between today and tomorrow. Afterwards, analyzing different techniques, I came to a simple conclusion. Our body is isolated from the outer world, and our consciousness, linked to the body, is isolated too. However, a human being has various layers of consciousness. The youngest layer is linked with the physical body. It is born and dies with it, and depends on it. On the other hand, there are layers of consciousness that are primary in respect to the body. Accordingly, the body depends on them. These layers are connected not to the body, but to the entire universe. When we begin interacting with them, our higher abilities open up.

For this reason, since time immemorial there existed clandestine groups of people that tried to understand the universe within. In order to enter the subconscious it is necessary to still the body and mind with it. The Old Testament describes several situations when people fasted for a few days before a serious event. After this, their prayers materialized more quickly, and if they went to appeal to the King, their request was granted.

In India, if someone wanted to develop higher abilities, the key condition for this was the absence of family, children and sex. When Pythagoras admitted students into his academy, he offered each one to undergo a forty day fast. If the person could observe the fast easily, this meant that his soul was ready for detachment. Then he was given another test. He had to be silent for a few months, or sometimes even years.

A human being is a social creature, and communication takes a tremendous amount of energy. Not coincidentally, monks often took a vow of silence and solitude; became reclusive. In the school of Pythagoras, spiritual energy went into abilities and was used for the development and protection of one person. In the case of the monks, this energy was used for greater unity with God, and therefore for the development and salvation of many.

By the way, for a long time I did not understand why Christ went into in the wilderness for forty days, and why a forty day fast has always been considered optimal. This puzzle was solved recently. One patient told me a curious observation about learning to type on a typewriter. If a person learns typing for the duration of from twenty to thirty days, then after a while the skill is lost. If, however, a person practices typing for forty days or more, then regardless of the amount of time that passes, the skill remains.

I suddenly realized that forty days are also a code of access into the subconscious. Our memory must discard that which is not needed. However, if we maintain our effort or internal state for more than forty days it then goes into the subconscious and exists there indefinitely. If a person observes a strict fast for forty days, especially in the spring when the subconscious opens up, then for the entire remainder of the year he may rejoice and have his external desires fulfilled while internally remaining detached. Therefore, he will be able to resist becoming a slave to these desires and will not have to pay for human happiness.

A person who cannot forgive is a person incapable of accepting the past. This is a person who can sacrifice neither voluntarily nor involuntarily. Love and faith in God do not exist without sacrifice. Therefore, a person who does not know how to forgive and accept pain while maintaining unity with God is ill.

Psychologists conducted an unusual experiment. People of different social groups were asked one question, "Would you be able to forgive the people who crashed the airplanes into the Twin Towers in New York?" Some flatly replied, "No, never." All of them turned out to be seriously ill people. So, mankind tries to storm the subconscious, not in order to perfect the soul, but to provide for the needs of the body. However, there is a significant particularity. A harmful thought in the conscious mind harms one person and his body, while a harmful thought in the subconscious can harm the whole of humankind and the entire universe. It is probable that in such a case the universe will protect itself.

Twenty years ago I heard about the experiments conducted by a Chinese scientist in Khabarovsk. The whole universe is a collection of rhythms and fluctuations. Any process quantifies, that is, occurs in portions. This means that using wave technology it is possible to change the structure of any object, including living ones. I saw a photo of that smiling Chinese man. At that time he was seventy years old but looked forty.

He immigrated to Khabarovsk at the beginning of the Cultural Revolution and created a fairly simple technological apparatus. Treating chicken eggs with rays, he would turn them into duck eggs. His experimental rabbits gave birth to saber-toothed rabbits. Later, I had a conversation with a person who is considered the father of modern psychological weaponry, and he explained this phenomenon as follows:

Any process and any object has its primary resonant frequency, including DNA. If this wavelength is found, any desired information can be downloaded into the DNA of a living creature. In 1990, this person mysteriously and inexplicably disappeared. Several years later in New York, I read publications about his recent experiments. He had treated his ninety year old father, who had already lost all of his teeth, with the rays of information taken from a young man. After a while, his father grew new teeth and became several years younger. Moreover, he underwent a considerable physical change, acquiring a resemblance to his informational donor.

So after this inventor disappeared, I thought he had been killed. Later, I read in a newspaper that he now lived and worked in China. It is most likely that he was abducted by the Chinese secret services. This country, unlike Russia, knows how to value professionals. However, since the general population of China is polytheistic and the main ideology there is Communism, their accelerated technological progress may be fatal not only for China but for all mankind.

Actually, this looks strange. China, with it's ancient and high culture, was never particularly religious. The secret of this phenomenon, I think, is explained as follows. The tremendous information that mankind received seven or eight thousand years ago was conveyed in the Indian epics, and then recorded in the sacred books. In a processed and simplified way, this information reached the West, ensuring the flourishing of Mesopotamia, Ancient Egypt, Israel and ancient Greece. This same information crossed Tibet, and then turned up into the North-East, into China and later Japan.

On the highest level religion, philosophy and science become one and are united. If in the West higher knowledge came through religion, in Tibet and China knowledge entered through philosophy. Therefore, the traditional upbringing of the Chinese people provided the same knowledge of the universe and implementation of universal laws. Moral laws in China were always observed very strictly. Theft, namely corruption, in China is punishable by death. In Russia theft is called democracy, and the indulgence of corruption and theft is considered to be humanitarian.

I wonder whether Russia will be able to restore its destroyed feedback mechanism with the universe in time. From the perspective of the universe, the fate of a nation and of an individual is the same thing. First a person makes one mistake, then another; one moral offense, then another. However, all actions are always linked together and one action relentlessly pulls others behind it. This is called the law of karma.

All events are connected through time because of their common root. If a man has murdered or robbed someone and then tries to forget about it as if nothing has happened, this is a great illusion. These things do not leave the subconscious and he will continue killing and looting unconsciously.

Even if he donates huge amounts of money to the church, if a priest pardons his sins a hundred times, this man will still subconsciously remain a murderer. Only in the case of his personality's complete transformation can his subconscious change; only then may his so-called sins disappear.

Therefore, the suffering that Russia underwent during the Post-soviet period are quite logical. If you were ready to hate enemies, then receive illnesses! If you were eager to worship a piece of bread as your main happiness, get destitution! If you put a man on a pedestal as the highest entity in the universe, receive lies and betrayal from public officials. If you despised morality, get the current chaos.

I recall a quote by Friedrich Engels, "When it comes to the interests of the proletariat, there can be no question of morality and ethics." For Engels this idea was quite logical. After all, morals and ethics have no material expression, while the proletariat with its dictatorship was real leverage for world change. I remember how when I was still a little kid, I overheard rumors that the Chinese planned to be first in starting a nuclear war. According to the world's laws socialism had to win, so there was no need to delay the breakdown of capitalism. Socialism would definitely win in a nuclear war, and the faster it happened, the better.

Somehow, nobody even considered that our entire civilization might perish. The cause of death for all mankind could be just the single thought: socialism will definitely win, and capitalism will definitely die. When a human thought is elevated to the absolute, this always ends tragically. The claim to absolute truth and his own infallibility belonged to the most highly spiritual creature in the universe, and his transformation from angel to devil was a natural process.

Belief in the infallibility of Communist ideas killed socialism in the same way that the thesis of the Pope's infallibility is now killing Catholicism. People are made in such a way that they need to worship something or else they turn into animals or die. Released energy should be realized in the form of a goal, and all intermediate goals must merge into a single higher goal. If one's final goal is not the Creator, then man in all of his manifestations becomes the goal. However, the worship of even the most noble human qualities and ideas begins to smell of Satanism and self-destruction. The tragedy of Capitalism and Socialism is that they are twin brothers. Both worship human happiness. The only difference between them is that Capitalism worships today and Socialism worships tomorrow.

Capitalism worships individual consciousness, and is doomed for this reason. Individualism leads to the worship of human instincts. The pursuit of money, violence and sex are essential attributes of an individualistic mentality.

Socialism worships collective consciousness, trying to destroy individual consciousness. Today, many countries in South America once again focus on socialism, realizing that American capitalism has no future.

The appearance of socialism in China was a sign of a serious problem in this country. The spiritual impulse had begun to wane; philosophy and morality had receded into the background. There was an increase in individualism, in the same way as when it destroyed Sodom and Gomorrah. The socialism that appeared in China impeded these destructive tendencies. However, if there is no understanding of the world's laws (and socialism is a very primitive attempt to understand the laws of the universe), then any social system is short-lived.

There is a third path, which we now see in Arab countries. The priority of religion allows capitalism and socialism to complement each other, because the main goal is not the individual or the society, but faith in God. The economics and politics of Arabic countries prove their viability; nevertheless, this prosperity is also temporary.

In Europe, religion first gave impulse for significant spiritual growth, which was followed by rapid economic development. Next, the growth of civilization started to smother culture and religion. Therefore, the future of our planet belongs neither to Capitalism nor to Socialism. Perhaps it is only the unification of science and religion which could help civilization flourish and retain its moral framework.

In principle, the ideas of Communism were based on intuitive providence. People of the future would need to be kinder; they should not steal, plunder, or kill each other. Their energy would be directed into self-development instead of going into envy. They would be able to love and forgive. The opportunity to work would for them be an enormous happiness. In fact, all communist ideals are consistent with the Ten Commandments. Only the core of these commandments, belief in God, had been eliminated. It would be interesting to understand why?

There is only one answer. The idea of communism was an opposing alternative for a religion that had misunderstood and distorted the teachings of Christianity's founder. Communism tried to take the essence of the Old and New Testaments and discard surface layers that obscured the truth. However, in order for man of the future to appear as conceived by the Communists, he would have had to have one quality that would allow him to work happily and to give far more than receive.

This quality is energy. Who envies another person, wanting to take away another's wife, livestock and property? A person who does not have the energy to create these for himself. Who becomes used to stealing and looting? A person who is not accustomed to earning these for himself. It is much easier to take away from others than to create for yourself. Who will not respect their parents, look after them and forgive their weaknesses? Again, it is someone who doesn't have enough energy. Care, unselfishness and self-sacrifice require a lot of energy. Those who do not know how to forgive are those who do not know how to sacrifice. Sacrifice is voluntary loss. Painless sacrifice is only possible for those who have a high level of energy.

It turned out that those who began building communism did not have this level of energy. People did not want to work for free. As hard as authority tried to convince people that it was labor that created human beings, that work was great happiness, still nobody wanted to work. Work 'for the idea of it' did not become popular. People simply began to die from starvation. Lenin, despite all his ruthlessness, was forced to allow NEP, the New Economic Policy, according to which profits went not into a 'common pot' but to the individuals who had earned them.

I heard the following story: After the revolution, Fyodor Shalyapin, a famous Russian classical singer, was summoned to the theatre where he sang and told that from that day on he would be paid as much as the stage workers. The singer quietly agreed, and the next day came to work wearing work clothes and began helping the stagehands change decorations. "Fyodor Ivanovich, the concert is about to begin; you have to go on stage," the administration tried to hurry the singer. He replied, casually waving his hand, "Oh, let one of the workers sing!" When revolutionary citizens appealed to him, asking him to work for free, Shalyapin responded, "Only birds sing free of charge."

Actually even birds don't sing without a personal interest. I always loved the nightingale's song, and believed its trills to be the expressions of joy and happiness. It turns out that through his song the male marks the territory where he resides and which he controls. Singing is a demonstration of his power and energy, persuading a female bird of his potential. A bird's song creates an energetic atmosphere that helps him exist and procreate.

It seems that the topic of payment is clear. However, there is a curious observation: if a person is severely depressed and has a strengthening reluctance to live, he must find some kind of occupation or hobby and do it without payment. Then the depression will go away. Why is a person not supposed to make money in this case? I will explain: melancholy and depression represent a drop in internal energy. When a person begins to give energy, getting involved in something and not binding this flow of energy to a certain about of money, his energy balance is restored, and as a result the soul and body recover.

The more energy you give, the more energy comes. Why did the richest man on the planet donate half of his fortune to charity, deciding not to allow his children to inherit the other five or six billion and leaving them only one thousandth of his wealth? He did this because he realized that a huge amount of money would stall his children's energy, their further degeneration and death would follow.

Previously, money and material possessions were a guarantee of a person's survival. Now the world has changed. People's basic needs are protected. If a nation provides each child with equal security and education, then the accumulation of huge capital for children becomes somewhat pointless. Then the point of gathering wealth begins to change radically. Work, the accumulation of spiritual and material wealth, becomes the reason and the means of giving more and more energy.

Why is a man happy when he builds his house? He thinks in this way, "I will be secure and comfortable." Actually, he is happy because in this situation he needs to give a lot of energy; physical, spiritual, and creative. However, when the house is built and the man moves in, his feeling of happiness disappears. Therefore, we experience much more happiness when we are in the process of striving towards our dream. Actually, that which we believe to be our goal, that is, the achievement of material and spiritual wealth, is just a means to give away as much creative energy as possible.

However, giving large amounts of energy without replenishing it is fatally dangerous and in order for energy to be restored we must constantly carry the feeling of love in our souls. Without faith in God this is impossible. Therefore, whether we are working the soil in order to plant tomatoes, earning money to buy an apartment, buying a car, or building a comfortable home; these are actually all means of achieving greater love in our souls, means for realizing God in ourselves. Perhaps the time will soon come when the act of working will be much more important than getting paid for this work. In the past, such an attitude was characteristic of only a few, but soon it will be the need of every person, and every person who has earned a lot of money will at the end of his life transfer this money to the state and donate to society, so as not to deprive his children of their chance at happiness.

I walk on the promenade, along a river in an awakening city, trying to drive away all extraneous thoughts. I listen again to the birds singing and look at the trees and houses illuminated by the rising sun. I pass small restaurants. Earlier, in Singapore there were very cheap electronic products, and thousands of Russian merchandise dealers flocked here. Now, in Russia it is possible to buy electronics which are more reliable and cheaper. Singapore has become an expensive city. Over the past two or three years, the prices in restaurants have doubled. The industrial work which was still here not long ago has now shifted to China. Its time for the citizens of Singapore to think about a new concept for development.

I continue my walk. After a while I come to a big bridge and turn back. Garbage collectors are appearing on the streets. Lovers of fitness are doing their morning jogs. I again walk through the underground passage, but the beggar is no longer there. Forty minutes have passed since we parted. I look at his aura again and see a strange picture: his energy field is in a whirl. I notice powerful lines indicating the abasement of all of his attachments. For some reason, he is going through a spontaneous purification. I have often seen this same picture in patients before an appointment. As soon as a person has bought a ticket for one of my lectures or seminars, all of his inner dirt begins rapidly coming from all of the soul's nooks and carnies. Relatives begin getting sick, children start experiencing nausea, diarrhea, and high temperatures out of the blue. They are showered with troubles, and illnesses sharpen. I've seen similar processes in people who go to church. The procedure of the soul's purification can be very painful. The main thing is to accept it at its earliest stages.

I remember an amazing situation that took place yesterday. Having visited a large store, I needed to return to my hotel. I decided to use the local subway. When I went down into the station I was pleasantly surprised: it was a clean, beautiful, spacious place. I needed to go to the Chinese district. I saw a woman walking with a pretty young girl beside her, and asked them how to find my train. They pointed me in the right direction. With a crowd of locals, we took the escalator down. The girl came up to me once again and showed me the direction in which to go; I thanked her. I noticed that she was dressed simply, yet very elegantly. We heard the buzz of an approaching train. Suddenly, I saw the same girl hurrying back to me. She apologized and signed that I had to go in the opposite direction. I smiled, thanked her, and patted her on the arm.

Then, on the train, I had a strange feeling. Something had happened; I could not detach myself from the situation. I looked at the girl's energy field on a subtle plane. Before our meeting, she had not looked great: in her field I saw children incapable of living. The girl would have failed to accept the purification necessary for her children to be born. Her beauty and grace had closed this opportunity to her. Children are our future, and we will be able to receive this future only when we will be able to accept its loss. Beauty, spirituality, ideals are all linked to the future.

On a subconscious level, a very beautiful and spiritual woman worships the future much more strongly. Accepting the collapse of her future, a betrayal, or the humiliation of her beauty is much harder for such a woman then for others. Beauty and spirituality are also a form of wealth that can hurt us if we lack sufficient love. Most likely, she wouldn't have been given the chance to marry, or her husband would have turned out to be infertile, or would have refused to have children, or she herself would have been infertile. Otherwise, in order for her children to be born, automatically there would have been a purification which she would have been unable to overcome. She could have fallen ill, died, or her family could have fallen apart. Her child could have been born sick or died.

I did not allow myself to see very subtle levels in order to avoid regret, worry and sympathy. On subtler planes there are fewer options, less human will and more predestination. The most striking thing was that during the ten minutes of our communication, her energy field had been completely purified, and now she could have a family and children without it being dangerous. I knew that the illusion of complete recovery would not last long. Fifteen minutes later someone would push the girl, would say something wrong, and everything would return to normal. I was interested in when this would happen; how long she would be able maintain her state.

It was not for nothing that when the first Association of Parapsychology was founded in the Soviet Union, I was asked to work in the field of Remote Diagnostics. My ability to see over distance what happened in the soul of another person helped me to observe cause and effect quite distant from one another. I could construct a single picture out of separate fragments. Strange, but the emotional state of 'soaring' in this girl was still there and did not disappear even after twenty or thirty minutes. In forty minutes something incomprehensible started to happen. Her field began to deform and vibrate. The source of the vibrations was located in very subtle planes, seemingly in other worlds. It seemed that these were the souls of her descendants.

Usually, the souls of children reside in the underworld, but exceptional people's descendants often come from other worlds. Suddenly I realized what was going on. If a person's soul experiences a burst of love and holds onto it for more than 40 minutes, then the opportunity arises to purify the soul deeply. Dirt comes up from the depths of the soul, and a painful purification begins, impossible to undergo without the feelings of love. If the person doesn't reject the feeling of love in a time of pain and agony, then the purification of the soul becomes complete and spreads to the person's descendants.

It was likely that this girl would have harmonious and exceptional descendants, and so her amount of love had to be greater, and her purification had to happen on a bigger scale. I continued to observe her field, thinking that it would be unlikely for her to withstand the purification at this time. She would likely yield to negative emotions emerging from nowhere. Possibly, she could experience melancholy, old resentments and regrets. Then there might be a dramatic increase of seemingly reasonable criticism towards men, and she would yield to these emotions, forget about love, and the purification process would stop immediately. Then, the future death of her children would again appear in her field, as well as misunderstandings on the part of men, strange quarrels, and separations. After this there would be illness, the absence of children and family, and prolonged loneliness. I tried to drive away all of these thoughts, switching to something else, but the thought of the young Chinese girl would not leave my memory. After seven hours I couldn't resist, looked at her from a distance, and was amazed. Her field was still shining; it was smooth and bright. It seemed that she had managed to pass the test.

Emotion is an energy field. Emotion permeates throughout the entire universe. Whether we think about the living or the dead, we always come into emotional contact with them. I am very experienced in handling painful situations; otherwise, I wouldn't be able to help other people and write books. Perhaps, this girl had intuitively felt my support and so was able to pass the challenges that had been insurmountable for her in the past. I looked at her field a week later; the field was still harmonious. After a while I noticed a soul of a harmonious child in her field.

However, and now I'm going along the embankment in Singapore and looking at the field of the beggar I had wished a happy New Year. I see that he is sliding into his past condition. His field has changed, but improvement had happened to about twenty or thirty percent. He experienced melancholy, irritation and unhappiness at his fate. Probably he succumbed to these feelings, and the purification process had immediately stopped. Maybe it was because the girl had taken care of me and given energy, while the beggar only received my gift and rejoiced, who knows? In any case, contact with the feeling of love, joy and care does not go away without leaving a trace.

In the Old Testament, God speaks to the people, *"Keeping mercy for thousands, forgiving iniquity and transgression and sin, and that will by no means clear the guilty; visiting the iniquity of the fathers upon the children, and upon the children's children, unto the third and to the fourth generation."* (Exodus 34:7). This means that there is a lot more mercy than punishment. In language of science, the inertia of love is hundreds or thousands of times greater than the inertia of anger, hatred and resentment. What are resentment, hatred and judgment? They are rejection of the purification preceding love and following it. In order to give birth to Jesus Christ, His mother too had to undergo purification. A woman who became pregnant out of wedlock in ancient Israel had no chance of survival. She should have been stoned to death.

On one end of the scales, there was love and signs from above, and beside them possible death, abuse and humiliation. On the other side of the scales there was the possibility of getting rid of the dangerous pregnancy, and a happy, peaceful life. This woman chose love and belief in God; this turned out to be more important to her than her instincts and her life. Through Jesus Christ, information came that can allow our current civilization to acquire a new future. Christ was able to renounce his future for the sake of Divine love, and passed along the knowledge that was necessary for the people. For His mother, love and belief in God were also more important than the future and her own life.

At least once in each lifetime,the soul of each human being must make the major choice: what is more important, love for God or the future? Not only Christians but also Muslims believe in Christ as Savior, because He not only said, but also throughout his life showed the extent to which love for God is more important than any human happiness. He who is willing to lose his future for the sake of love, will acquire it. Every person should be put in this situation. Now a time is coming when the whole of humanity must make this choice.

I turn away from the embankment and come to the hotel. Later today, a taxi will take me to a ferry. Forty-five minutes later the ferry will arrive at Bintan Island, where it will be possible to sunbathe and relax. In my soul I experience joy and elation. I positively like Singapore; I don't know yet know that when I check my luggage in at Singapore Customs, two bottles of excellent cognac bought in Duty Free will be stolen. At first I will be angry and judgmental of those who did it. Then there will be irritation and accusation of myself; what a fool I had been for not putting all of my valuables in my carry-on case! Then I will look at the situation as at an opportunity to sacrifice. I obviously have yet to overcome the topic of security and justice. Higher forces kindly offer me an opportunity to take care of my soul, and I respond by puffing and becoming irritated. Truth to be told, I will not remain this way for long. Much less than I would have been a few years ago. In such cases, a positive dynamic is what is most important, right?

Chapter 5

A Meeting in Togliatti

On the eve of the seminar in Togliatti I wake up in the middle of the night. At first, I do not understand what has happened. Then I realize: my condition has worsened dramatically. Life is slowly leaving my body. Energy is quietly and smoothly disappearing.

I have become used to responding to the first signs of danger. What do we normally do when we feel bad? Our habitual reaction is to suppress this sensation, to put it aside. We treat it as an enemy, a disease; but it is a warning.

A simple tip: if an aggressive emotion or an inner discomfort begins, detach yourself from everything and pray. Then, perhaps, the fatal danger that has brushed against you will decrease by many times.

I begin to pray, trying to detach myself from my condition; otherwise diagnosis will not work. I used to think that that betrayal was simply a collapse of one's ideals and future. It turns out that it is a much deeper process. First, unity with the world crumbles, and then the second phase begins: the destruction of one's future and destiny. If at this moment you preserve love for God, then you are able to accept the destruction of unity with this world and divine energy enters the soul.

The collapse of unity occurs at the moment of one's death, especially when it is painful. If in this moment one preserves love and aspiration towards God, then the soul is cleansed. However, the intensity of love needs to be very high, otherwise it is not possible to withstand.

What is the character of a human being? It is the sum of our reactions to the surrounding world. These reactions are determined by how we perceive ourselves. If I am vulnerable, I try to respond to any situation with love and goodwill. If I am strong and secure, I respond with aggression. If I am an important authority, I react to being hurt with anger and irritation. If I am a small child, I react to being hurt by crying. If I am love, I react to being hurt with love. If even for a moment the divine 'I' becomes a reality for us, aggressive emotions disappear. Therefore, it is very important to feel ourselves as love, materialized. Then any of our harsh external actions will educate and help others rather than destroying them.

It seems that the essence of Christianity is to feel the Divine within. In Judaism, God is outside human beings. Sin is also outside people; in their behavior and lifestyles. Christianity is a manual on how to experience God inside. Sin, according to the Christianity, is inside a person. As soon as we lose the Divinity within us, we make the first step toward sin. The angel who lost his sense of the divine self became the devil. He decided that his 'I' was his consciousness, mind, will and ability.

In order for the Divine to move into the human soul and become reality, it is necessary for love to flow continuously without being impaired by judgment, resentment or melancholy. One of the highest barriers that are difficult to overcome by people short on love is betrayal from close ones and loved ones, the feeling of a near or imminent death, and agonizing death itself, especially an unfair death. However, if in such moments our love doesn't shake, then the purification of the soul can be complete and divine love will come, along with new energy and a new future. In order to feel that your real self is Divine, the intensity of love must be such that there is no more dependency on any of the levels of human happiness.

A new future is approaching humankind. In order to obtain it, it is necessary not to depend on it. If you learn to love one who betrayed you realizing that he had nothing to do with it, if your love isn't shaken when you learn that you will die tomorrow, if people and destiny treat you unfairly and your dreams and hopes collapse yet your love for God not only endures, but also increases, then you will survive the changes that will soon begin.

One of the letters that I received during a seminar was about a woman that for ten years had read my books and tried to put herself in order, and only recently was diagnosed with cancer. If it were not for diagnosis, I would have made the following logical conclusion: my research had failed to help her. When I looked at her energy field, I realized what had happened. She had managed to work on herself, but when work on her children and grandchildren started, her soul had been unable to accept this. Her rejection gave birth to aggression, which was paused by disease. In order to purify not only ourselves, but also our children and grandchildren, the intensity of our love needs to be from 90 to 100 units. To purify our own soul, twenty units is enough. By the way, the woman had the latter amount.

Sometimes, after a baptism in the Orthodox Church little children can get sick or even die, and the better the energy of the church, the more problems can arise in a child with a dark soul. People who have inner aggression towards love feel poorly in church; even to the point of losing consciousness. For this reason, many do not go to church, justifying this with external causes. Soon, the whole of earth will become a temple, and only those who have learned to love will survive in this energy.

At the beginning of a seminar people do inner work, and I go through letters. A woman who was being treated for infertility. Her note was short but impressive. First, her infertility was treated by two healers who died afterwards. During her pregnancy she was diagnosed by a healer, who also died. Prior to conception she had sessions of medical massage. However, the extreme pains did not go away until she gave birth to a baby girl. The woman asked me whether this was related to the birth of the baby or not. I looked at the intensity of love in her soul. The figure was obscured with three crosses. The woman's soul was absolutely incapable of giving; her field showed complete consumerism. I tried to calculate her willingness to give: seven or eight times worse than fatal. Nature did not want such a woman to have a child, and she simply did not have the energy to reproduce. The healers had pumped the woman with energy, her consumerism had intensified, and the baby's soul had darkened. For their help with bringing such a child into the world, the healers had paid with their lives.

What is happiness for any living creature? It is the realization of their program, the satisfaction of their instincts. All of us are tiny, dimming systems, and any new information contradicts our internal picture of the world, brings pain, forces us to change and adapt. Happiness is only half of our capacity for development. Discomfort, misfortune, unhappiness are also modes of processing new information.

Current medicine tied human beings to their bodies. Just like science, it began working in the mode of polytheism, worshiping physicality and destroying the soul; distracting people from stress and orienting them towards stability and calm. Modern civilization's ability to adapt began to decline dramatically.

Our main mechanism of adaptation is our feelings, our anguish upon interacting with the new. The possibilities of consciousness are very small, as are the abilities of the body. We think that our consciousness is rapidly growing, changing the world around us. However, we ourselves do not change; our feelings are at a standstill. In fact, we have not progressed far beyond the people who lived two thousand years ago.

Our polite manners and exterior gloss, that which we call a civilized upbringing are only forms, which must be the result of our soul's development and the love that comes from faith in God. However, if the form actively develops and looks great, this doesn't mean that the content is also doing great. The content might still die. Oneness with God can be lost without us noticing. Love and our feeling of unity with the entire world can leave our soul unnoticed. Meanwhile, form will continue to evolve, rejoice, and delight, ignorant of the agony that is about to begin.

How many times were a variety of cataclysms and the end of the world predicted, and the predictions haven't materialized. Probably, people simply needed this sensation. The sense of near death makes us forget about the body and remember the soul. In our present situation, perhaps for the first time in human history, a cataclysm is not only possible. As scary as it sounds, it will be necessary for the salvation of our dying civilization!

People have convinced themselves that they believe in God, but at the same time they violate the Commandments, without which it is impossible to reach God. Our modern life is in essence theatre, in which monotheism has turned into ordinary polytheism; where Divine laws no longer exist leaving only human laws; where people no longer worship love, but rather their consciousness, ideals and goals and are ready to exterminate love, life, and faith in God for their sake.

I suddenly recall a conversation I had with a woman. Her story was very interesting.

"I devoted myself completely to work," she told me, "and then noticed that I had become weaker. I was having problems with my thyroid gland. It came to the point where I could not even wash a towel; I just could not lift my arms. I was supposed to fly to Moscow for surgery but had no energy at all. Then my friends took me to an old Korean healer who taught acupuncture. In a few days he put me on my feet, but said that if I did not change my lifestyle and my attitude towards people, nobody would be able to help me. I then realized that this was my last chance and started feeling better."

"Could you explain what happened to me?" She asked.

"Yes, I'll explain," I promised, "But first, would you be able to arrange a meeting with this healer for me? There are so few true professionals."

"You are several years late," she replied. "He has already died. A year before his death he told me that he would die soon, and wished to die in the place he had been born, that is, in Kazakhstan. He sold his house at a low price and left. A year later he died."

"So he was able to predict that his death would come soon?" I asked.

She shrugged her shoulders and looked at the sky. "Yes, he said that there was death which could be avoided, and there was unavoidable death. The first signs of it appear ten years earlier, then three years, and then one year before death."

"Did he talk about what these signs look like?" I asked with curiosity.

She looked at me from the corner of her eye and smiled. "He said that it was better for ordinary people not to know. It can be harmful for a weak soul." "Please tell me," she asked suddenly, "Should one try to avoid a preventable death, if it is in fact sent from above and purifies the soul?"

"What do you think?"

The woman shrugged her shoulders. "I don't see much of a difference."

"There is a difference," I said, "A substantial difference. Imagine that you study at school for ten years, pass the final exams, and leave its walls. This is inescapable death. Now imagine that after the third grade you are expelled for disorderly conduct and bad grades. This is a death which you could have prevented. However, in both cases, you find yourself outside the school."

"And what does death at a young age mean, in your opinion? Can it be inescapable?"

"Sometimes students are allowed to take their examinations without attending classes, within a short period of time. However, the quality of their education usually suffers. In Judaism, it is thought that a baby lamb should live for at least one day before it is slain; in other words, it must live a life, albeit a very short one. It is forbidden to take its life completely, depriving it of a future, or else the future will be taken from the one who has slaughtered it.

Sometimes the soul is burdened with sins to such a degree that the person has no right to live. However, the soul is purified only through love and suffering. In this case, abortions happen or babies live a short life and die. This chance to purify the soul at least a little bit should of course be used. Overall, inescapable death is linked with old age."

I see a question in the woman's eyes, and change the subject. "Now, let's turn to your issue. You are a smart and beautiful woman, and you have a high level of energy. If there is no belief in God then all the latter qualities can become dangerous, because a strong mind, beauty, and powerful feelings; all of these increase one's possibility of coming into contact with the future and, accordingly, to govern it. You probably haven't succeeded in your personal life, have you?" I asked, looking her in the eye.

"Yes, I had two marriages, and both were unsuccessful. Moreover, the second marriage was even worse; my husband turned out to be a drug addict. Why do you ask?"

"The more educated, beautiful and intelligent a woman is, the more difficult it is for her to accept the collapse of her ideals; injustice, the humiliation of her highest desires. However, if she is a believer and her love for God is more important to her than the future, then the destruction of her future in the form of spirituality, beauty, principles, and ideals will be easy for her to overcome. The smaller her amount of love, the more painful the purifying process must be. A woman idealist must get an imperfect man and learn to love him as he is.

The more this man humiliates the woman with his appearance, behavior, and emotional condition, the greater the woman's chance to feel love and hold it above her ideals, that is, the future. If a woman internally rejects her imperfect husband she will receive an imperfect child. If she is unable to treat her husband as a child, that is, with continuous love and also the strictness that is needed for education, then this mechanism will inevitably be activated, and she will have a sick child. If a child is sick in his body or his soul, the future will be oppressed in either case, and in the subconscious, love will inevitably begin to win over spirituality.

So when your personal life didn't work out, you devoted yourself completely to work and it become the main goal for you.

A person who worships the future always possesses certain characteristic qualities. He sets a certain goal in the future and pursues it, destroying everything around him. Because love and life are secondary for him, such a person is usually merciless towards himself and others. The stronger his concentration on the goal, the more powerful his internal mechanism destroying those who get in the way of this goal. The more spiritual the person is, the crueler he becomes.

In your case, your cruelty turned against you. The worship of higher feelings leads to jealousy and impatience with close people not only at home, but also at work. You tried to escape family problems through work, replaced jealousy with pride, but gradually problems began accumulating there as well. Our body started to lose energy, and health problems began."

By the way, I once held a consultation with a woman whose thyroid gland was the size of a fist. When she read my books, she tried to inwardly release control of her situation, and the firm growth immediately became softer and then decreased to the size of a dove's egg. She then came to another consultation. "Stop inwardly controlling and managing your husband," I said to her. "You do not live by love, but rather by your principles and ideals. For this reason, your husband is a thief within law."

When we try to change and teach another person relying on ideals, principles and objectives, we begin to demand, reproach, accuse and judge them. To change another person one must constantly hold the feeling of love in one's soul. Only then, requests or severe measures may have results.

I mechanically shuffle another note in my hands. I try to forget extraneous thoughts, and inspect the text. A young woman writes that she was always able to predict future events. She always felt what was going to happen. "It is hard for me remove my fear of the future," she has written. I can see that this is an insurmountable problem for her. She had felt her diagnosis before the doctors told her about it. A year and a half ago her temperature rose suddenly to forty degrees, and stayed this way for quite a long time. An ambulance came to the house several times, but the doctors were unable to identify what could be the cause of such a high temperature. She had neither rashes, nor a cold or flu. Everything was normal, but the high temperature ran for about a week. At this time, she felt something clearly, and then the feeling turned into a thought which came to her mind, "I have AIDS." Two weeks later her lymph nodes enlarged, and after a month she was diagnosed with HIV infection.

The woman writes that she has had HIV for about a year and a half; the concentration of the virus in her blood is nearing the stage of AIDS. Her condition already requires treatment. Doctors are not able to explain this, saying only that everybody has different physiological systems. Someone lives with HIV for twenty years and still does not need treatment, while someone else begins to deteriorate after a year. Medicine cannot explain what the speed of transition from the initial infection to its last stage depends on. The woman writes that she neither did drugs nor had indiscriminate relationships. The cause of the disease is still incomprehensible to her. At the end of her letter she writes that she only recently realized that the cause of the problem was not physical.

Phrases from this letter continue to rise up in my mind. I take a pen and draw her energy field for myself, for clarity. The field is bad. There is not only her own possible death, but also the death of her children. Her aggression towards men is high; very bad indeed. Ok, I try to look at the situation from another angle; maybe there is a chance somewhere there. Her willingness to accept a traumatic situation is closed. Her reserve of future is closed. Her intensity of the feeling of love is closed.

I have not seen such a serious situation for a long time. Most likely, she would have died in any case. Love and energy have left her soul. The dying form, that is, the body, was looking for any illness because it was a chance for survival. If the soul is awakened in time, it will have time to warm the body up and give it a chance of survival.

I look again at the audience, pondering. Why does AIDS most often appear in drug addicts, homosexuals, and prostitutes? If, as usual, we take the physical model as our foundation, this is because of promiscuity, unsanitary conditions, and a perverse attitude to the body. This is the reason and most important; that is, an imperfect person is the main distributor of the disease. The fact that a person who becomes a drug addict, homosexual, or immoral person is one who cannot accept the collapse of his future is something that scientists don't even suspect. If love leaves the soul, energy and the immune system leave with it. The more advanced medications become, the more complex the diseases.

First, we lose sight of Divine will and love for God as the primary means of our existence. Then we begin internally fighting with any unpleasant situation, forgetting that any situation is part of the universe. The more the Divine is lost to us, the more strongly our soul reaches for the external happiness enveloping our body. Internal aggression grows and energy drops. The only thing that can save a dying soul is the sick body that modern medicine is trying unsuccessfully to cure of all diseases.

I wonder what the woman's internal state is like after beginning her inner work. I look at her field and see a very good picture: her acceptance of a traumatic situation is already positive. In her soul, love is also beginning to wake up. Instead of dirty, torn, square stains, her aura has become a pearly golden. Only a strong black spot near her head remains. These are her children. So, she has passed aggression towards love on to them quite strongly. This means that either she did not want to live in her youth when treated with a collapse of the future, or she had judged or hated her loved one or father. I now understood why the stage of infection moved into the stage of serious illness so quickly: not just the woman has this unfortunate condition, but also her children. Bringing the children into shape will be more difficult.

Of course, after the seminar, the love felt by its participants will decrease. Some people worry about this and panic; however, they will never forget this feeling. Just as a committed crime never leaves the depths of our soul and permanently and invisibly damages us until we atone for it with illness or misfortune, so the awakening of unconditional love is never forgotten, and later saves our soul in difficult situations. The feeling we have felt is an advance. Later, this same path must be repeated independently, there is simply no other way.

I am distracted from my thoughts by another female participant's question. "Tell me, if at the moment somebody hurts me and I feel pain, I do not experience hate or judgement towards this man does this mean that I have gone through a painful situation correctly?"

I shake my head. "No. If you use all of your effort to remove hatred and resentment towards another person, you merely shift the arrow towards yourself. Simply put, it will not be the other person who dies, but you. This is because you will be killing not the man but yourself.

If you do not sustain the feeling of love, pain will not push you in the direction of God. You will then have to tread on someone else or on yourself. It is necessary to understand that any unpleasant situation pushes you towards love and God; any pleasure also. What do we normally do? When we receive pleasure, we internally worship it, cling to it and become dependent on it; when receiving discomfort, we despise and tread on others or ourselves. Worship and hatred are twin sisters. Love has no place here.

In order to preserve love in a time of pain and loss, it is necessary to look at the whole world as we would at a child. The greater the loss, the more intense our love needs to be in order to endure it. If you lose your wallet and tell yourself, "I still preserve love in my soul," you will be able to do this. If however you have been hurt by a loved one, then this phrase in itself will probably not be of much help. The intensity of love and energy will need to be significantly higher.

To overcome the collapse of the future, which may look like the death of a loved one, the collapse of goals and hopes, an insult of our most sacred feelings, our intensity of love needs to be completely different. If it is insufficient, we will lose the future, together with health and life. It must be admitted that at this time, there are not so many of those who can overcome the collapse of the future. For this, it is necessary to continue loving the surrounding world no matter how cruel it might seem, to love the person who betrays you or who treats you unjustly. That is, any reason for impeding love must disappear.

This mechanism of salvation has already been known for two thousand years. It is described in the New Testament. Nevertheless, over the past two millennia we did not accumulate but rather lost love. Perhaps, in order to understand the great truths, it is not enough to just suffer. We need find ourselves on the edge of death, where a person faces either death, or a transformation from being a 'reasoning' person into being a 'loving' person. Everyone will make this choice in favor of love, many probably after their physical death. Some during the course of severe diseases. For a small number this choice will happen without them noticing, though I have mainly come in contact with the first category of people."

"In principle, this is logical," I ponder, shaking my head. "People come to me when therapists, psychiatrists and surgeons can no longer help them."

Another question comes from the audience. A young woman anxiously tells her story.

"I have been reading your books for about 10 years, and my life and health have changed for the better. There are only two problems that continue to concern me. First, my husband and I often argue and sometimes fight, and afterwards find reconciliation difficult. Second, my husband has a hernia in his spine, which causes him excruciating pain. Could you please explain what the problem is?

One second is enough to see the entire picture. "You have learned to go through painful situations correctly. You have learned to forgive and accept what has happened. However, you have not been able to overcome your dependence on the future. There is still not enough love in your soul. In conflicts with your husband, you should find a common point of view which matches both his and your interests. In order for two opposites, two conflicting sides, to find a solution reliance on love must be greater than reliance on principles. You still lack this. Each of you defends your own future, your principles and worldview. Opposites should not fuse but they should not explode either, destroying one another. When there is a lack of love in the soul, spouses are not able to build harmonious relationships. They either fuse, depending on each other, or the slightest conflict immediately leads a fist fight, with the desire to win rather than reconcile."

"Maybe you don't understand this," I say, looking at the young woman, "But internally you are absolutely unwilling to yield to your husband. A woman needs to preserve love, not righteousness. A sense of righteousness automatically leads to the judgment of others. Judgment in a woman leads to sick and dying children, or lack thereof."

The woman nods contentedly and sits down. However, after a while, she raises her hand again and asks another question. "So you say, God, love, and all that stuff..." she started.

"I do not say that," I stop her. "For me, God and love were never all that stuff.

She is embarrassed and waves her hand. "Well alright. All of this is understandable but illusionary. On the other hand, devilries, sects of satanists, are a very strong and powerful reality. They gain strength and win at everything around them."

I want to reply to her, but suddenly my spine feels as if it has been pierced with two needles. I realize that I have judged her. If I do not overcome this, I will also get a couple of intervertebral hernias. I mentally repeat to myself, "I do not have righteousness, and she does not have guilt." That which we often see as someone's fault is, actually another person's delusion. That which we believe to be our righteousness is in reality our delusion. For the Jews surrounding Christ, truth was their own righteousness. For Him, the truth was love. I slowly calm down, and the pain disappears.

Those for whom the future overshadows love, will always see the devil as a much more realistic figure than the Creator, although in actuality there is no devil. Devilry is an infection that parasites on our souls, depriving us of the feeling of love; it is needed in the same way as disease, which reminds a person about his inner lack of wellbeing.

Remember, Christ said that if a single demon is cast out, seven worse demons will come in its place. If the body lacks energy, then while curing one disease you will discover several new ones. If there is no love in the soul then however many demons you cast out, they will only keep multiplying. Therefore, the apparent strength of satanic sects, of devilry, is simply people's disregard of the Commandments given to them by God. It is the gradual and inconspicuous loss of love in the soul.

In a person sick with AIDS, the slightest infection can lead to the most severe diseases. Devilry is a disease of the soul. By the way, recently in a TV program, one priest said that from the viewpoint of Christianity, the majority of patients in mental hospitals were possessed. I think he is absolutely right. Those who worship their conscience, which is closely linked to the future, must lose at least a part in order not to lose everything. Numerous mental illnesses which have blossomed in recent years are an unconscious attempt to survive when there is almost no future left.

Everybody sees only the first stage of a soul's death; delight in one's consciousness, goals, and desires. Few people see how the second stage looks. It looks like the deterioration of consciousness; the lack of goals, desires, weakness of will, and futility. While there is still love in the soul, but consciousness is held as a much higher priority, we see power, strength, and all of the signs of devilry. As soon as love leaves the soul there begins a rapid disintegration of consciousness, desire, and strength.

It is difficult to see the relationship between cause and effect on a surface level. Recall the movie 'Apocalypse Now.' First, a person feels his undeniable superiority over others; then he decides that he can control the destinies of others and then declares himself a god. Afterwards, his soul 'becomes crazy,' although his consciousness remains crystal clear. Then he feels that soon his psyche will also go mad; the consciousness he worships. Devilry comes to a logical conclusion. Sensing that his consciousness will soon disintegrate, the man asks to be killed, because a physical death to him as a military man seems much less painful than the disintegration of consciousness.

I part my hands, implying that my response is complete.

"Life works in such an interesting way," I think. "One woman has solid health, while all of the people around her die. Another woman's surroundings are alright , but she herself is dying. The process is one and the same, at different stages of its development."

Life works in such an interesting way! Any process splits into two halves through the interaction of the future and the past. First, worshiping something, a person looks to the future. Then, regretting and hating someone, he turns to the past. Any process is a swinging pendulum, alternating between the future and the past. Perhaps, the law of pairs stems from this process. If we try to translate the language of the Old Testament into our modern one, the main 'crime' was committed by the devil, or rather by the angel who began worshipping not the Creator but the future, that is, consciousness, ability, and his own spirituality. Therefore, the opposite of the devil is not God, but a mad, weak-willed and impotent creature.

The spiritual and the material are two halves of a single process, in which the spiritual represents the future, and the material represents the past. Often a person who has been worshipping spirituality for a long time feels himself becoming insane and changes his idol; begins worshiping the material. He stops being an idealist, believing in hard pragmatism. Money, stability, and prosperity become the main purpose of his life. When this aspiration also infiltrates his soul the person begins to get sick and die; he suddenly realizes that the spiritual and material, left and right, are part of one whole. This whole is what people call love for the Creator, and it is the intensity of this feeling that determines whether a person will survive when the world of familiar relationships starts crumbling around him.

In my first books, I outlined what must not be done. All of this can be expressed very simply: One must not kill love, no matter how valid the excuse is. When we try to abandon this feeling, to subjugate it, govern and discredit it, we commit the most important sin in the universe.

Where does the concept of 'good and evil' come from? From the notion of 'good' and 'bad.' Where do the notions of 'good' and 'bad' come from? From seeing the future. Here is an example to illustrate. There was practically no food left in the village come spring, but there was a reserve for the next planting season. One of the villagers said, "Our children are hungry, let's eat the seeds!" Another man said, "We need to suffer, to endure the hunger, so that we can survive next year." "You are a wicked man," shouted the first villager. "You want us to suffer; you want our children to die!" "No, you're wicked," replies the second villager, "because you are submitting to your desires. Today you get full to the brim, and tomorrow you will die of hunger." However, the first villager was very convincing. Furthermore, the hunger felt by the villagers was on his side, so he won and arranged a big feast for everybody. The following winter the entire village died out.

The notions of 'good' and 'evil' differ from each other here only in their degree of penetration into the future. An unspiritual man lives by the interests of his body and stomach, and makes decisions that seem brilliant to him, and benefit his stomach in all respects. It turns out later that these decisions have led to disaster. Subconsciously, we call that 'good' which contributes to our protection and survival, and that 'evil' which leads to our destruction. The farther we look into the future, that is, modulate what will happen, the greater our chances of survival. However, worship of the future can result in a loss of love for God, and the loss of that same future.

There was, only recently, a popular Russian phrase: "It was meant well, but it turned out as usual." There is an even more ancient wisdom; "The road to hell is paved with good intentions." Christ said, *Man does not live on bread alone,* "(Matthew 4:4) and then added that nor does he live by tomorrow. He who worships a piece of bread will die tomorrow. He who worships the future will die the day after tomorrow. Worshiping the material or spiritual reduces the soul's contact with its Source and leads to self-destruction.

The biblical story of Adam and Eve allegorically describes the emergence of life in the universe and shows the main dangers that life presents for people. Why is it the snake that takes on the role of the tempter?

Because a snake is inconspicuous, hidden, and invisible in everyday life. This means that the loss of the Divine can occur inconspicuously. More importantly, the snake is a symbol of wisdom; that is to say, it seems to be the bearer of the tendency to worship the future and spirituality.

In this way, life has two dangers: the worship of the spiritual and the worship of the material. The loss of oneness with the Creator leads a person to worshiping one of the currents of time: first the future, that is the spiritual, then the past, that is the material. In this way, he heads towards destruction if there is no return to God. In principle, this is a repetition of the eternal cycle of the universe: the Divine becomes the spiritual; the spiritual turns into the material; the material either breaks up or spiritualizes, gradually transforming itself into the Divine and returning to the Source.

There is an ancient Russian proverb which my mother liked repeating, "Youth eats gilded gingerbread and thinks that it is daily bread." A child is born with a very powerful impulse of love and unity with the Creator. Gradually, developing, he loses this impulse. That which he used to have in abundance, with age he must create himself; that is, the intensity of love in each person must increase throughout the course of their lives.

In childhood there is only one problem: not to kill love. Then the next problem appears: how to increase love in the soul. Next, it is necessary to address the most important challenge: how to feel love continuously so that it becomes our natural condition, our main self.

Just as any process in the universe, the human life pulsates. Occasionally time compresses in such a way that a few days can affect our entire life: these are the moments of puberty, first love, conception and the appearance of children into the world. That which happens in our souls during these periods defines our destiny and our survival in the following years.

These same processes take place in the destinies of nations, states, and our current civilization. Recently many people have noticed that time has condensed and all processes have accelerated. I wonder what state we will be in as we go through this period of time.

Chapter 6

Consultations

Today I will conduct telephone consultations. I will have to examine several people. I like diagnosing by voice even more, it's easier to detach myself and see what is essential. My main task is to turn all logical explanations into feelings. If the memory of a consultation transforms in the patient's memory into a set of advice, the chances of overcoming disease are very small. Deep personal change is impossible without engaging the subconscious. That which we call instinct, emotion, personality and habit are all the subconscious.

If you have *realized* that you need to change, you practically have no chance of changing. However, if you *feel* that you need to change, you will change. Many have noticed a curious phenomenon: if a person says, "Starting from tomorrow, I will stop smoking or overeating," this tomorrow never comes; the day constantly shifts further and further into the future because interaction with tomorrow happens through consciousness.

Our feelings, that is the subconscious, exist in the present time; if you do not begin to change now, right at this moment, it is unlikely that you will succeed. Hence, the expression, "Don't put off for tomorrow that which you can do today."

Reality, factual events, first occur on a subtle plane and then materialize on the physical level. Our subconscious is linked with the whole universe and with the subtle realms, so people with strong intuition, that is with an open subconscious, can intuit events ahead of time even though they often cannot govern them, because they are unable to change themselves.

Yesterday I watched a documentary on TV about the disaster of 9/11. An elderly man talked about his tragedy. A month before his son's death, he had felt and sensed the inevitability of the young man's death. Three weeks later, the father took away his son's car key. He had enjoyed risky driving. The father hoped that this would save his son's life, and he had started taking the subway to get to work. On September 11, 2001, the young man had taken his familiar subway route. His office was on the 104th floor of one of the World Trade Center towers. The plane with the terrorists rammed the building in the section of the 75/80 floors. Those who were upstairs had no chance of survival, even theoretically. The son's body was never found.

The subconscious feels death, or rather knows about it, and sometimes this is shown through physical signs. I remember an unusual story told to me by a woman at a session:

"One day, walking around the city I noticed a small group of people in an underground passage. I approached them, and looked over someone's shoulder. It turned out that there was a man on a bench reading palms. He was a chiromancer. The payment was small, and I was curious what he would say to me. My turn came up. I approached the man, extending my hand. He did not look at my face, only at my palms, and told me everything about who I was and what had happened to me in the past. "You have one child, a daughter, and she will soon die. You should be ready for this," said the man. I had always noticed signs of trouble in my daughter, but I had not attached any importance to them. I do not remember how I left the underground passage and came home. I sobbed and read your books for three days, and on the fourth day I went back to the same place. The chiromancer was there. I got in line again and when it was my turn, approached him. Once again, he did not look at my face, but only at the palms, and again repeated my destiny word by word; what had happened and what was happening in the present. 'You have an outstanding daughter,' he said. 'She has a strong character, and a great future is awaiting her.' 'Three days ago, you told me that my daughter would die. Here, on this very spot you looked at my palm and told me about this.' He took my hands again and carefully examined their patterns. After some silence, he said, 'I am responsible for what I see, at the present moment there is no death of your daughter."

When I hear stories like this I am no longer surprised. I don't experience triumph and pride because my studies are repeatedly proven by life. I see these processes around me constantly. A person who changes his emotions simultaneously changes his subconscious; he changes his character, destiny, and the entire course of future events. He is able to change the destiny and health not only of his children, but also of distant relatives. That is, the information of the Bible is affirmed: one saint can save thousands. There is a small stipulation: if they are willing to follow him. The willingness to follow a holy man is the willingness to practice self-restraint, accept pain. It is the willingness to sacrifice, to forgive, to put love for the Creator in the foreground and be ready to periodically sacrifice human happiness for Him. Love must win not only over money, but also over our desires, our will and our concept of justice.

In modern man, the notion of self-restraint is gradually atrophying. "Take everything from life!" scream television advertisements. "Do not stop for anything!" affirm characters from popular literature. An increasingly popular toast at celebrations is, "For us to have everything and pay for nothing!" A person learns to live by his desires, concentrating on them. The obliteration of any obstacles for the sake of one's desires is called success, winning the competition. Those who teach this 'shave' big money off of their 'lost sheep.' Big money is made not by those who encourage restraint, but by those who condone desires and debauchery. By the way, what is sexual debauchery? It is complete permissiveness of desires coupled with a complete rejection of love and morality. Each person slides into the quagmire of worshipping desires in his own way, yet the result is approximately the same for everybody.

I remember the story of another of my patients. "My daughter has severe epilepsy," she told me. "The disease started when the girl turned one; now she is two. I started reading your books, but nonetheless my daughter nearly died. Once, in front of my eyes, her face became covered with spots and turned blue. The ambulance arrived in time and the girl was taken to the emergency room. The doctors honestly said that it was the end for her and told me to prepare myself for the funeral! I realized that I had lost everything. I had no hope in anything or anyone. I simply turned to God and said, 'Lord, I accept your Will; I accept whatever is going to happen, and I will always preserve my love for You!' Suddenly, my daughter's state began dramatically improving. It's hard to believe, but in one day the life line on her palm increased by many times. Earlier, the line had been very short."

The mother also talked about herself. "It is difficult for me to pray, although I am a strong willed woman, a Master of Sports, and I have two higher educations. Since childhood, all of my desires materialized; if I wanted something I would always accomplish it. I find it very difficult to normally relate to fools and weaklings; to this day I am displeased with my husband even to the point of rage and this is very difficult for me to overcome."

"Hold on," I said to the woman. "Tell me about your daughter's character."

The woman paused, remembering. "To be honest, she is irreconcilable: if something is not her way she begins to scratch and bite. Once, my brother paid us a visit; he also has incidental epilepsy. When he came up to her she suddenly fell into a rage, attacked him, tried to bite him, and then began to scratch herself. By the way, could you explain why this happened?"

"There was a common resonance of her energy with the energy field of your brother," I explained. "An emotion has an energetic structure and resonates with similar fields."

Our desires are tied to the body and serve its interests. Naturally, the interests of our body do not coincide with the whole universe; therefore, in our desires there is always conflict with the surrounding world and other people. One person's desires are always in conflict with the desires of another person because they have different bodies. Conflict is only absent in the place where there are no bodies and there is absolute unity in love for God. The more a person believes in God, the stronger his ability to love and to give; the easier he can solve any conflicts. For this it is necessary to educate yourself and others. A compromise is a mutual sacrifice by both sides. Restraint, the restriction of desire, is powerful leverage for development. The more selfish our desires anchored to the body, the more aggressively we will behave towards other people. When, while taking care of myself, I will consider the interests of people around me at the same time, my aggression will be noticeably reduced. Belief in God, enabling us to feel unity with the whole universe, enables us find the perfect balance between our personal interests and the interests of the surrounding world. Broadening our communication with the surrounding world, we develop ourselves as identities. This is the paradox of development: the more a person satisfies his desires, the faster his desires degenerate and weaken. This was the way that the sexual revolution of the 1960s led Europe to impotence, infertility, and homosexuality. The more aggressively a person defends his desires, that is, the interests of his body and his life, the narrower his options become; he begins to get ill, his abilities decline, his sexuality weakens, and his destiny falls apart.

"A child is like a magnifying glass. Supporting and enhancing processes happening in his parents' souls, both good and bad. In your daughter's soul, the pathological process created by you has increased to the limit, and so a braking mechanism has taken effect. For the soul to survive, the body must go through pain."

The woman paused and then stopped me. "I have often seen people who are hateful and judgmental, and nevertheless live well and are in excellent health. Why aren't they punished by God?"

"If you run with all your might into a wall and hit your head, will your leg also suffer?"

"Why does the leg have to do with anything?"

"Because you are a united organism. If wrong conclusions made by your head lead you towards death, your legs will suffer also. Externally you and your daughter have different bodies, but on a subtle level you are a united whole, and your daughter will pay for your wrong conduct and your emotions.

Recently, I heard a curious fact on TV. The serial killer Chikatilo revealed his family's secret to his son: he had had a brother, whom his parents had killed and eaten during a period of starvation. After this, something had turned over in Chikatilo's soul. So, if someone beats his head against a wall his whole body will be affected, albeit not immediately. Why the mechanism of punishment stretches for years, decades, and sometimes many lives is not our concern. The level on which we make a transgression corresponds to the time needed for us to work the wrongdoing off. First our children depend on our sins; then we get sick and die for them, atoning for our guilt. If a fault remains unpunished it will be repeated in strengthened form until it is corrected; either by human or divine law.

"Do you know what the difference is?" I said, addressing the woman, "Divine laws unfold slowly and inevitably, and for the misconduct and sin of one person, all of his descendants are destroyed. The universal laws listed in the Divine Commandments provide an understanding of sin and expedite punishment, helping prevent the demise of society or an individual's descendants through his early punishment. Morality helps a person be virtuous, not because of his fear of punishment, but because of the power of his own beliefs.

The supreme law of the evolution of the universe corresponds to the main cycle of its evolution. The universe originated by the will of the Creator, strives towards Him and will return to Him. To put it quite simply, the essence of development is an expanding love for God and increasing unity with Him. He who professes this principle, a believer, takes more care of his soul than of his body, sees Divine will in everything without judging the world and people surrounding him, doesn't envy, steal, plunder and kill, because this is not consistent with his inner direction.

A person who succumbs to judgement and envy, who constantly blames others, gradually loses his sense of the Divine in his soul, and so begins the slow process of extinction which sometimes takes effect after many years or generations."

I become lost in thought again, and memories move to the background. Now the phone will ring, and I will have to listen carefully to a patient's problems, explain the cause for each problem, bring everything together into one point, and turn it all into the feeling of love, helping the person overcome himself.

The telephone rings and I tune in. The call is from the father of a child who has serious problems; the diagnosis is myopathy, muscle atrophy. Muscular dystrophy usually lasts until the person can no longer breathe; next comes death by suffocation. I remember consulting a woman with similar problems. She could no longer walk and her husband carried her to me in his arms. When she appeared in my office a year later I couldn't recognize her; she was a different person. She got to the fifth floor without help and felt fine.

I recalled another patient who could barely climb to the apartment where I was then seeing patients. His face had a greenish tint. "You live high up," he said.

He walked into the apartment without removing his shoes. His bodyguards stayed outside the door.

"I am diagnosed with seven illnesses, all of them fatal," he said. "I have a feeling that soon I will be killed, so I always keep a gun under the pillow."

"If you are destined to die a gun will not protect you. If you want to survive, forget human logic," I said.

A month later he came to see me again. He walked up the stairs easily, and his face was no longer greenish. His situation was better, and I let him know this.

A most curious thing happened two or three years later. A young man came to see me, and asked me to examine his son; suddenly my acquaintance, who had been present at the consultation two years ago, took me aside and said in a low voice, "Remember you saw a wealthy man, who had seven illnesses? That is him, only he looks ten years younger."

It was hard for me to remember, but it turned out that this was that very man. His energy was completely different: he was soft, calm, shy, and his child's energy field was quite good.

I detach myself from memories, and turn back to my patient.

"I will not look at your child at this time," I say. "I will diagnose you and your wife. If you're fine then it's your child's personal karma; however, this is unlikely. Furthermore, personal karma usually coincides with family karma. I have no doubt that you've placed a 'heavy load' on your child."

The patient gives the names, and I examine their energy fields. Earlier, I would have spent a long time diagnosing the child and then the parents; after that I would have looked at which events had destructively influenced the child's soul and body. However, I later realized that if you try to take the stairs three or four steps at a time, it is impossible to climb them. Because diagnosis and treatment go hand in hand, the task must be addressed in phases. Before surmounting the first step, it is useless to think about the second. The first step is accepting a traumatic situation. Without aspiration towards God, complete acceptance of Divine will, the understanding that any situation leads to love and to God; if a person has not learned at least a little how to preserve love in any situation, accepting a traumatic situation is impossible for him.

The process unfolds in a simple scheme that I have already described many times. If you aren't able to accept purification through people, you will get a disease. If you don't accept it through illness, you will get death. It's strange, but the father's degree for accepting a traumatic situation is high, like that of a healthy person. The child's mother, however, is a catastrophe. Her inner acceptance of painful situations is way below zero.

"Have you read my books?" I ask the man.

"Yes, I have read all of the books, listened to the tapes and worked on myself."

I nod. This had been clear right away, even with superficial diagnosis.

"And what about your wife?" I ask. There was a pause.

"She was interested," he answers uncertainly.

"She should become seriously interested if she wants to help her child. What is myopathy?" I ask the father. "It is the destruction of muscles, or self destruction. What is a self destruction? It is the result of a program of self elimination. What is a self elimination? It is a program of hatred towards the world and towards people, which has turned against the person himself. What is aggression towards people? It is the rejection of traumatic situations, and this rejection is the inability to preserve love towards God when experiencing loss, pain, and offense. Why can't a person preserve love towards God? Because for him unity with the world is more important than oneness with God. Human happiness for him is a greater pleasure than love towards God. So, if your wife will not decide to change your child's chances of survival are slim."

"Her relatives had similar illnesses," says the man suddenly.

"Its harder to overcome a family's karma but still there is no other way. Your wife needs to learn how to love and forgive. By the way, you also have a share in the child's illness," I say, "Even though you have learned to accept any situation."

"Of course," he replies. "There could be something left over from past years."

"Actually no, you continue to behave incorrectly," I say. "You create too much comfort and excessive stability for your wife; internally, you worship your relationship with her, therefore amplifying her dependence on human happiness. A woman subconsciously intensifies a man's philosophy and his inner orientation. For a man, the right world paradigm is much more important than for a woman. For millennia, women stayed at home, caring for and educating children, while men built altars and temples and performed religious rituals. The right perception of the world in which the Divine was in first place and the human was secondary was passed on to women, and they multiplied it in themselves and their children."

Before, I could not understand why while mothers were responsible for children's illnesses, fathers got ill and died much more often. Only recently I understood that we are responsible for those we've corrupted. You must give your wife and children continuous love; it is a Divine feeling and should not be interrupted. However human happiness must follow a sinusoid wave. Today it is necessary to be soft, and tomorrow harsh. Yesterday the relationship was colder, and today it is warmer. Only the Divine can be eternal. When we try to make human happiness stable and eternal, we begin to become attached to it and the pain of losing it becomes unbearable. Because stability is death for the material world, worshiping human happiness leads to hidden aggression towards the entire surrounding world.

We see how what we love disseminates and wastes away. Trying to protect that which we love, we look for guilty parties and show aggression towards the world. However, since the main source of transformation, development and destruction in the universe is the Creator, ultimately we target our aggression at Him. Next, of course, there is a turnaround and self-destruction. Everything which causes aggression towards God must be destroyed.

Therefore, comprehending God a person goes through several stages. First, it is necessary to feel and understand that any situation leads to God and love, to learn how to internally accept the will of God. Then it is necessary to learn how to love. One should discard anything that interferes with love: regrets about the past and worries about the future. One must accept everything that has happened and will happen. People and events must disappear, and in everything we should see only the will of God. It is human consciousness that sees degradation and development, left and right, good and bad, while Divine logic embraces both sides of the coin simultaneously. We are destined to return to the Divine; both the worst sinner and the finest saint. If on the human level there are people in the right and in the wrong, as well as the personal responsibility of each individual, then on the karmic level there are no people; there are only tendencies passing through generations. This can be called the karma of a kin.

In India, there is a saying, "There are no people, only ideas." On this level, the personal will of each person is very relative. On this level, a person who has offended us is not only a scoundrel but is also our savior. On the most important level, the Divine plane, there are no villains; there is only Divine will. Here we are all already forgiven in the past and saved in the future and we have the right to one feeling only: love. Human will does not exist here as well as a person's individuality. Thus, Christ said, *"And not a hair of your head shall perish,"* (Luke 21:18) without God's will.

Since we are Divine in essence but also have a material body, we are destined to function in multiple logics. Human logic is a tiny part of Divine logic; it is necessary for the maintenance and development of the body but must always be secondary, in the same way that the interests of a cell are always secondary to that of the organism. This is the normal cycle development and existence in the universe.

Now let's turn to practice. In a nutshell, here is what you need to do. First you must form the correct world paradigm in yourself; second, you need to help your wife acquire the Divine. Somewhere thorns and somewhere roses. On average, profound change takes from two to six months."

"After that will it be possible to arrange a consultation with you?" asks the man.

"It is up to you," I respond. "You have my telephone number and appointments are available."

The telephone rings once again.

"I have already been to see you," says the woman. "Basically everything is ok with me. I would like to ask you a few questions, as I am curious how I am doing in terms of my inner work."

"Your results in changing yourself aren't bad," I say, "But your inner worship of human happiness, spirituality, and ideals has not yet been overcome. In a past life your spirituality began overtaking love, and an attachment to the highest human values developed, therefore, in this life accepting the collapse of ideals and the future has been an insurmountable challenge for you since childhood. In such cases, the chances of having children are very slim."

"I have no children," she reminds me."

I nod. "Yes, this matches the diagnosis. Ask your questions."

"I have been overweight since childhood," says the woman. "No matter how hard I try to lose weight, I still can't. Moreover, since childhood I have seen prophetic dreams, and everything I saw would come true. Furthermore, for almost a year the little finger on my right hand keeps going numb." She pauses.

"Continue," I tell her. "And then I will respond to everything."

"Recently I have had a strange feeling. When I am outdoors, and see groves, trees, I suddenly experience a deep sadness and melancholy. Strange, I once experienced joy and now it's quite the opposite. Another strange thing: lately, I can't eat fish. Recently I had a very strange dream. I wanted to eat fish; I stared at a cooked fish for a long time, enjoyed looking at it and craved it. I began to eat the fish, and suddenly I did not feel good; next, I was surprised to see how a finger on my right hand fell off. Shall I continue?" she asks.

"Yes!"

"After I read your books, I began helping people, even unintentionally. A girl at work would have a headache, come over and stand next to me, and the headache would go away. Little by little, others began complaining about their various pains. I said to them that we were not in a hospital, and asked them to let me work. Moreover, as soon I would empathize with someone, it would immediately stick to me. Things would stick to me most when I felt melancholy, but I didn't always feel sick from helping others. Sometimes, on the contrary, I would feel lighter. That is all, i suppose," says the woman.

"Everything you've said can be reduced to what we began talking about," I start explaining. "Because your spiritual potential is very high your contact with subtle planes is enhanced, hence the spontaneous clairvoyance in your dreams. Because ever since childhood you haven't been able to accept injustice and the collapse of the future, your inner protest has been turning into self-destruction, and in women self destruction is often blocked through being overweight.

The right hand is related to the future, especially the pinkie, and if it started to get numb, this means that you will be unable to accept situations that will happen in the near future. Groves and trees evoking a feeling of melancholy is your premonition of the natural cataclysms that will happen in the future. Since internally you aren't able to accept them you experience depression, while the numb finger impedes your vision of the future. Simply put, the more the finger will get numb the less melancholy you will experience in your soul, and if you fail to overcome this emotion you will be protected against depression by a serious illness.

In your subconscious, a fish is a symbol of human happiness and survival. It is probable that in a past life you lived near the sea, and fish was your life source. Now, in order to overcome the destruction of your unity with the world and accept future troubles you need to rise above human happiness, and so you develop allergies to whatever binds you to life.

The dream you saw means the following: if you do not make a decisive step towards the Divine, putting aside consciousness and life and experiencing them as secondary, then human happiness in the form of a fish will poison your life, and you will either experience a great loss, misfortune, or an incurable illness. A lost finger is hard to put back, so most likely the dream was a hint that you have little time left, so you must do your inner work and change yourself more intensely.

The fact that the girls at work feel better next to you reflects your strong spiritual potential and also your definite responsibility for the destinies of those around you. Recall the phrase, 'To whom much is given, much is expected of.' It is not a good idea to enable the human desire to get well; one shouldn't pass one's sins onto other people. First, a person must overcome his own problems and change independently."

"Do you know what the most dangerous thing is for you?" I ask the woman. "It is your inability to live through emotion. Spirituality is linked to consciousness and the future. When Jesus said, '*Do not worry about tomorrow,*' *(Matthew 6:25)* or '*Blessed are the meek, for they will inherit the earth,*' *(Matthew 5:5)* what he meant by this was the same as what the people of Ancient India meant when they said, 'The main enemy of human beings is thought.' You have probably heard the phrase, 'The devil knocks on the door to the head and God on the door to the heart.'

In order to see the Divine in everything it is necessary to stop consciousness. We perceive the Divine only with our feelings, with our subconscious. When a human soul is excessively attached to the physical body and its needs, more specifically to desires and consciousness, then touching the Divine is a very painful process. It is even possible to die if purification happens too fast.

Why does belief in God begin with sacrifice? Because without detachment from human life it is impossible to endure contact with the Divine. By the way, abstinence and self-restriction are also sacrifices. We have become used to the idea that self-limitation in desires, food, and sex is already sainthood. However, we must limit ourselves in consciousness as well. Only love is without limitations. "You have good changes," I tell the woman. "You need to take one more step. Your soul must make a choice: what is more important for you, unity with the world or the unity with God?"

In a few minutes the next patient calls. His voice is familiar to me; I try to remember and he helps me.

"Remember when my baby daughter was born I asked you to be her godfather?"

This scene from the past flashes in my memory and I remember everything.

"What's the matter?" I ask him. "Is something wrong with the child?"

"The problem is with me," he says, "And it is very serious. After the birth of my daughter I became attracted to another woman, and the feeling was very strong. In your books I read that one should follow one's feeling of love, so I left my wife. I regularly visit the child and have a friendly relationship with my ex-wife, but I don't want to live with her. The woman and I had a mutual attraction, and a very serious relationship: I felt as though I had taken flight when I met her, but later problems began. She tortures herself and me, and we can't be together. We suffered for over a year, and then she decided to part ways with me. She met another man, left town, and immediately became ill; developed hernias in her intervertebral discs. The relationship with the other man also failed; she was not able to stay with him. We have now restored our relationship, and once again it is continuous suffering. I have a feeling of complete hopelessness, as if I have been stunned and thrown away. The meaning of everything is lost and blunt melancholy has begun. Tell me, what can I do?"

I think, looking ahead of me. It turns out that my phrase, "Follow love and do not think about anything" is understood differently by everybody. For most people, love is a sexual feeling, or the admiration of beauty, or just an attraction towards another person. Simply put it is consumption; receiving happiness and joy. Consumption is always dependence, and dependence is pain and loss.

Typically, a love triangle appears when a man worships a woman's beauty, sensuality, and sexuality. Periodically we need to undergo the process of separating the human and the Divine. This happens through painful human relationships, and the more we are attached to human happiness, the more pain our soul feels when we are in love. "I wonder why is he being purified so seriously?" I think. "This purification is happening on the very edge of his capabilities."

"What's your daughter's name?" I ask him.

Once he says her name, everything becomes clear to me. The girl's energy field is shrinking. She is unable to accept the collapse of her unity with the world, the humiliation of human love, and the collapse of her destiny. In order to save her, her parents need to change internally. Their aspiration towards God and the intensity of their love needs to be significantly higher, and there needs to be a lot of pain; enough to save their child.

"You are now being given the easiest, most enjoyable, albeit most painful opportunity to help your daughter," I tell the father. "Do not leave this woman, strive towards love, continue to suffer and feel pain. You need this. If you fail to help your child it is possible that you will simply be destroyed, even without a serious illness. During previous consultations, I did not see how strongly you worshiped your loved one. This was in the depths of your subconscious, and when your baby was born everything hidden became apparent. Go back to your wife, trying not to traumatize her with a demonstrative relationship with the other woman. It sounds strange, but you love your wife more than this woman. You couldn't be allowed to know this. If such a purification were given to you through your family and your wife, you would not have been able to withstand it. This way you have some small support, so the traumatic situation on the side can work to help your daughter. You have not yet found real support. When during any physical pain and loss your soul will instinctively turn to God, the suffering will be smaller and shorter."

"But why should I return to my wife?" the man asks suddenly.

"For you, love is inextricably linked to beauty and sexuality. Sexuality is an animal feeling; it is necessary for procreation. In order to transform an animal into a human being, sexual feeling should be turned into friendliness; that is to say that if a woman has put you down as a man, or doesn't attract you which is in principle the same thing, you need to treat her as a friend or a sister. If a person has become used to sacrificing, restricting himself, and refraining, then the transformation of sexual energy into a warm relationship becomes easy and painless. Then, if your wife becomes sexually unattractive to you for a while, the warm friendly feeling still remains.

Next, in order for the Divine to be awakened in a person, the human part of him must be humbled. If a woman intentionally or unintentionally humbles a man's friendly feelings, then his human feelings need move to the Divine level, so that he will continue to love her with the love of a parent. He must continue to love her no matter what; no matter who she is or what she does.

We are animals and live by our instincts, and simultaneously we are human beings and develop our feelings and consciousness, and at the same time we carry the Divine inside of us. We love and are able to love with Divine Love, and sexual, friendly and divine feelings are always present inside of us. Why do women paint their lips and dress up beautifully? In order to kindle sexual feelings in men, and then turn these feelings into human, friendly emotions.

Sexual attraction and the desire to possess are transformed into a desire to help the woman, to take care of her, to do noble things for her, to be smart and willful, to achieve much in life and so on. If a woman is not only beautiful, but her love is permeated with love, care, and gentleness, then one's human feeling is transformed into a divine one, and a man wants to sacrifice himself for this love. Then he will continue to love her even if she becomes disabled, loses her beauty, ages, or dies. In the divine, love no longer depends on the outside world. Love itself starts to create this world.

Then our loved one then begins to feel better; becomes stronger, smarter, younger. What is a vulgarly dressed woman? If she wears excessively bright lip color, underlining her sexuality, the animal energy in the men around her no longer transforms into anything. If a man experiences a very strong sexual feeling and it doesn't transform into anything, instead simply swelling, he either will rape this woman to get release, will become seriously ill, or his energy of survival will need to drop several times; in other words his sexual drive will diminish to impotency.

In this way, it is possible to draw a direct correlation between the sexual revolution and the sharp drop in the sexual potency of European men. Now, even western doctors have noticed that women who dress up provocatively often become infertile, have low hormone levels, and develop polyps, tumors, and cysts of the uterus and fallopian tubes. Doctors say that hormonal overexcitement and constant nerve overloads cause disruption and destruction of main human functions. To some degree I think the doctors are correct, but this is also one of the causes.

A man who often uses the services of prostitutes tends to also become impotent. However decently a prostitute dresses, all of her energy is oriented towards a purely physiological act, the only purpose of which is pleasure. Therefore eventually the pleasure begins to devour love; the body begins to devour the soul, and the soul naturally begins to weaken and collapse. So when a man renounces the Divine and human in himself and becomes an animal, God punishes him. The reason that circumcision is mandatory in Judaism and Islam is in order to prevent a believer from masturbation. The pseudo-religious western world currently teaches children to masturbate, calling this sexual education and saying that masturbation is healthy; that it reduces stress, decreases the amount of rape and instances of juvenile aggression. I was told that in Israeli schools this subject is taught everywhere. In many countries, though following surface decency, people lose faith in God and leave behind their higher morals. The process of transformation from animal to human being is very painful. It is as difficult for a man as sustaining a feeling of warmth towards a woman who has debased his masculinity.

Those who build a family primarily on animal, sexual relationships are ultimately doomed to first experience serious problems and then the family's collapse. Take a look at what is happening now in Russia, especially among the famous and wealthy. A wife becomes a little older and her husband immediately throws himself into the arms of a young woman and marries her. It is pure paganism, animal behavior, and still the person calls himself a believer and speaks from the stage about love, beauty, morality, and so on. On the outside there is complete order while inside the soul there is emptiness.

Western countries, realizing the depth of the disaster, are attempting to turn back. To some extent, the spread of AIDS spurs this process: nature itself helps to impede human degradation. Why are frequent sexual relationships before marriage dangerous? During puberty, a girl accumulates a huge amount of energy later to be used not only for the formation of her future baby's body, but also in shaping the baby's character, destiny, abilities, and talents. For all of this, energy is required. Now imagine that all of this energy is transferred into pure sexual pleasure, without the girl wanting to conceive, meaning that she doesn't want to give energy to her future child. The more she concentrates on sexual enjoyment, the more afraid she is of becoming pregnant. It turns out that for a young woman, each such sexual act is a program which rejects her future children. At the same time, all of her energy goes not into the development of the spiritual and physical abilities of the future child, but into her concentration on pleasure and desire. Later, the woman begins to want a baby, but is unable to give birth to one. Animal emotion is full to the limit, and there is no energy left for human and Divine emotion.

Nature protects itself from such children. They can't live in a highly developed society; they can feel comfortable only in primitive society. This means that given our current moral standard, either our civilization will perish or women will stop giving birth. Thus, the end may be quick or it may come slowly, "as requested by the client." I recall a scene from a popular movie. The main character is asked, "Do you want to be killed quickly or do you want to suffer?" He looks up in the sky and answers, "I would prefer to suffer."

"So I wish you the same," I address the man. "In a woman you should first see the Divine; that is, perceive and love her as a child. Maybe you should even see her as a sick child, because then you will need to give her more love, and having less expectations of support from her in the future, you will have less self-interest. Next, you need to love the woman as a friend and companion, and only then as a sexual partner. When you learn to love her as I am describing, all your problems will be resolved easily and naturally."

We say goodbye and I hang up the phone.

The consultations were over. My head is buzzing. Strangely, consultations are becoming more and more difficult for me. Probably, this is so I focus more on writing books; perhaps this is the reason. Recently, a woman told me a story on the phone about a woman who tried to make an appointment with me. Her daughter was in a coma, The situation was very serious.

"Have you read his books and watched his videos?" my friend asked. "No!"

"Then you will not be able to make an appointment with him."

"But I can't watch his lectures because I am sitting in the hospital next to my dying daughter."

"He will not see you," my friend answered. "Read his books!"

The mother of the sick girl asked someone to bring my books to the hospital. She read the first book and there was drastic improvement in her daughter's condition. The mother got excited and put the books aside. The daughter's condition became worse again. The mother began to read the books again, more seriously, and the daughter came out of the coma, recovered, and was released from the hospital. I think that this was one of the best consultations I could conduct.

Chapter 7

Fishing

Our airplane's already been flying for two hours. First, we flew from Moscow to Frankfurt; then we transferred to another flight that is taking my friends and I to an island where we plan to fish. Ten more hours ahead of us.

We do not notice how the subtle threads of attachment, worry, and concern sap our energy. Any journey is a break from familiar connections. If you have the right attitude towards a journey, the energy that had previously been wasted can be channeled into conceiving new ideas, into bringing the soul and body to order.

I remember the story of an elderly couple who lived in the United States. The wife had inoperable cancer and the husband had a serious case of diabetes. Instead of a slow demise, the retired couple preferred a romantic trip with an unknown end. They spent all their money on this, even what was saved for the funerals. They travelled for about a year, and when they came home, it turned out that both were healthy.

We become accustomed to everything, including our errors. Our subconscious forgets nothing and often a wrong attitude towards the world, accumulated over the years, leads to an ever increasing loss of energy which goes unnoticed. Only with the arrival of serious illness, when the body rings the last alarm, we try to cope with the problem, often unsuccessfully.

Modern medicine doesn't allow a person to die, but does not help him recover either. Such a person is an ideal client for the growing pharmaceutical industry. Lately, I have noticed with interest the way that medicine has become similar to show business. Since ancient times, any merchant has known that if he invests more money into his product than he will make from its sale, he will go broke. Success in business is determined by a simple formula: one must strive to invest as little money and effort into the business and gain as much profit as possible. The greater the profit, the faster and more active the growth of the business. The material world has been confirming the veracity of this law for thousands of years. However, the human soul lives by different laws.

Art, which is linked to the soul and reflects its development, must abide by the soul's laws. The basic principle of art is to give a lot more than one receives. Art connects religion with science. Art evolves by following religious postulates, which contain a huge potential for altruism. However, if art is placed on a conveyor belt and turned into a craft, the laws of the material world, namely the laws of business, begin to take over. Love, sacrifice, altruism, the desire to make people happy, unity of all things; without these art can't survive. The soul is nourished by a higher energy from the Source, and it receives only when it gives, like a spring.

The materialistic western world has made art into a business, yet the mechanism that works very well in the material field has begun to kill art, and with it, the soul. The world of consumerism has spread its psychology on all spheres of human activity. Medical care has also gradually turned into show business.

An artist creates a piece of art to help another person and to make them happy. For this, he offers much more energy than he consumes. The goal of a merchant is to make as much profit as possible on his product and to make himself happy. Contemporary show business treats the audience as a source of profit. Present day medicine has begun to treat patients the same way. Along with the concept of the soul, other concepts have moved aside such as compassion and unity. However, if a person's soul is sick, it is impossible to cure him. If the soul is unwell, the consciousness and the body can be treated without end. Without the concept of the soul, healing the body and spirit is doomed to turn into a profitable business.

The moral paralysis that swept over post-Soviet Russia, within a short period of time leading the country to disintegration, is imperceptibly gaining strength all over the world. Why is it that people don't want to notice this?

I contemplate this, looking out the airplane window. Far below, vague outlines of the coastline float by. We have left the territory of France behind, and now are flying over the Mediterranean Sea. I look over the endless marine expanse with detachment. I wonder, why did life originate in the ocean? Why, while existing in the subtle realm, was it able to realize itself in water? Probably, this is because the characteristics of water are very similar to the all-encompassing, unified field of the universe.

The universe, while expanding, remains an entirely whole and united being. On the most subtle level, it is a point where time, space and matter are a completely united whole. This principle of unity is reflected in any event that takes place in the universe. Any living being reinforces this principle while evolving. All of the water on our planet is a single substance due to its formless quality. Water 'remembers' any information. It can take a stable form at a low temperature, and can return to its previous liquefied state.

Particles in a vacuum are formed in the same way: at a lower internal energy, space is structured into a substance. In this way, the development of materialism points to the low level of energy in society as a whole. A person with a weak soul and small capacity for the future perceives the world as everlasting, unwavering, and strong. When content disappears, the person is forced to depend on form.

I begin to contemplate again, looking at the sea which is shining below in the reflected sunlight, "Why did Cain kill Abel?" For thousands of years, we have reiterated the same version: because he was envious. But then the question arises: what is envy, and why is it possible to kill because of it? Why did this envy result in the murder of a brother? Nothing is accidental in the Bible. Every parable is an encrypted message that must be unravelled. Why was it necessary to encrypt the huge body of information contained in the Bible?

I sink into thought, and gradually come to understand it clearly. Unprepared people were not able to approach the mountain where a meeting with the Divine was supposed to take place. Why can a person die when receiving higher knowledge? Why can contact with the truth be dangerous? To understand this, we first need to answer, "What is truth?"

Lets imagine ten apples are placed in front of a student, and the teacher asks, "How many apples will remain if I take four away?" The pupil answers, "Six will remain." The answer is correct. What is happening in the student's consciousness at this moment? Behind the number six there stands a particular chain of events. It is necessary first to imagine ten apples, then mentally remove four apples, and after this count the remaining apples. There is a shrinking of time in this process; a series of events is compressed into one point.

The teacher asks the pupil, "And what will happen if you bury an apple in the ground? What will happen in six months?"

"The apple will remain the ground," the student answers.

"This answer is not quite correct," the teacher says.

"Maybe it will simply rot?" the pupil guesses.

"This answer also cannot be true," the teacher says.

"Then, maybe the apple will sprout, and a new apple tree will appear?" the pupil adds.

"This may be," the teacher responds, "But in order for the answer to be closer to the truth, we must know the place where we bury the apple, the type of soil, and the climate. We need to know at what depth to bury the apple; we need to know whether the apple is rotten or healthy. Much depends on the time of year we plant it, on whether we have selected a shady or a sunny place, on whether wild animals can dig the apple out and eat it or not. And what if someone unexpectedly decides to build a house on this place?"

So, in order for the answer to be as true as possible, we must link together a large number of events that are taking place at different points in time. However, experience shows that many factors which we take into consideration mean little unless we forecast the future. When we examine the land and place, we assess the present. But whether there is going to be rain or frost, whether animals will eat the apple, or whether somebody will build a house here: all of these are questions posed to the future. What is the difference between mathematics and real life? In mathematics, the number of factors is clearly defined, while in real life it is indefinite.

Truth is the concrete relationship between cause and effect. When scientists try to make the material world the reason, they conclude that understanding truth is impossible. However, since ancient times prophets and seers have existed, whose prophesies have become reality. But it is impossible to consider all material factors... What is knowledge as a whole? It is the sum of the relationship of cause and effect in the present, and its forecasting into the future. Seers and prophets could not have been able to take complete information from the present. Therefore, there is one conclusion: they got it from the future.

Let's imagine a tree with a huge crown. Thousands of leaves grow on its branches, which fuse into a single trunk. In the same way, on the subtle plane the material world becomes more and more united. On these subtle planes time flows slowly; it compresses. In the same amount of time, it is possible to acquire much more information. The deeper a person penetrates into the subtle field, the more he learns about the world in the present and in the future. Absolutely complete information about what has happened, what is now, and what will happen in the universe is hidden in the point where the universe is absolutely united. Thus, the absolute truth in the universe is its Creator. Therefore, to understand the truth, it is necessary to deeply sense the subtle planes connecting us with the whole universe, and then feel absolute unity with the Creator.

Why can't most people come into contact with the truth? It turns out that in order to understand a process, we need the energy to link events together, as well as detachment from the narrow, surface spectrum of events. A person with weak energy becomes attached to a tiny, superficial line of events. Given a truer understanding, connected with a line of events on a level ten times deeper than usual, the person will have only two options: either to allow a great over-extension of energy in order to accept the truth and die, or to reject the truth under any pretext in order to survive.

The process of understanding the world is a progressive replacement of more and more capacious and accurate beliefs about the world, requiring increasing internal energy. Without love and detachment, It is impossible to increase one's inner energy. Through the feeling of love we receive higher energy, and through detachment we embrace an expanding spectrum of events. Without abstraction the thinking process is not possible. In order for the concept 'chair' to arise, we must simultaneously keep in mind dozens of options of what might be called 'chair.' We must detach ourselves from the external form, while at the same time maintaining internal unity with each of these possible chairs.

Abstraction is the strengthening of content and reduction of the relevance of form. For a person who is excessively attached, greedy, and incapable of love, contact with the truth can become dangerous. Therefore, a person who has renounced his attachments and seen the world as a whole has always been closer to the truth. The rest of the population has believed such people and followed them.

The truths in the Bible are encoded because human consciousness is not able to handle them straight out, and so the Bible brings people to realms reflecting these truths. When we try to interpret the Bible superficially and literally, we unwittingly cut off our opportunities for development and further understanding.

What is the mechanism of envy and why do people kill because of it? It seems that each criminal carries Cain's genes. In each of us, a crime invisibly matures. However, in one person this mechanism triggers, while in another person it can be constrained. Why was the first criminal of all people and all times unable to restrain himself? I spent a long time pondering the phenomenon of envy and came to the conclusion that at the base of this feeling there lies the loss of truth. The ultimate truth is love for the Creator. Through this feeling, we receive information about what is happening and what will happen in the universe. Thanks to this feeling, we are able to change and evolve without being destroyed. Through this feeling, we receive the higher energy needed to provide for the future.

The mechanism of envy is actually very straightforward: it is fear for our future. Fear is the result of worshiping the future. Because God accepted Abel's sacrifice, this meant that Abel had a bright and safe future. Cain on the other hand had no future. For the first criminal on

Earth, the future was more important than anything else, including his brother and his love towards God. Because the future became more important to him than love, he lost his higher energy. He began to lose the ability to change, evolve and provide for his future. Then, he took away the future of his brother. Having killed Abel, Cain tried to steal Abel's future for himself.

Any person who destroys his system of priorities, electing material and spiritual benefits as the main purpose in life, is doomed to extinction. This mechanism has been working in every person since the days of Cain. The idea of Communism is the idea of worshiping a bright future. The natural envy of those who had more gave rise to the desire to exterminate the rich. Worshiping a bright future, the Bolsheviks turned into 'Cains' and slaughtered their brothers by the tens of millions.

I become lost in thought, looking in front of me. At my consultations, I often see people with almost no future, people with devastating diagnoses: diabetes, cancer, schizophrenia, homosexuality, drug addiction. When there is no energy for the future, energy has to be taken away from the physical body. Not only can the body deteriorate, but destiny, relationships and consciousness often follow suit. However, before losing the future a person first becomes attached to it; worships it. Interesting, what does a person who worships the future look like?

Suddenly, I am distracted from my thoughts by a friend sitting nearby. "Ivanovich sent you his greetings," he says. "By the way, he has lost everything; everything was taken away from him."

"What happened?" I ask.

"Everything as usual: they falsified documents, bribed a judge and took his business and land away from him. Of course you know," the friend gestures with his hands, "In the past, they killed and confiscated property, while now everything is done using the law."

"How is he feeling now?" I ask.

My friend smiles. "He is trying to accept the situation in the right way." Then he says. "Maybe I should pass something on to him from you?"

"Tell him this," I say, "At one time, he told me a story that happened to him while he was serving in Afghanistan. Once they were riding in an armored troop-carrier, and he, as the commander, was sitting in the front. Suddenly, he had an irresistible urge to sit in the back. A few seconds later, In the place where his head had been the armor of the vehicle was pierced by a shell. Back then, he himself changed his seat, and now his fate has hauled him away from danger."

"So he should not fight for his rights?"

"He can fight for his rights, but without changing his internal state, it is useless; he will simply be killed."

I see the puzzled expression in my friend's eyes and continue. "Imagine our mutual friend at two points of his life: a year ago and now. Mentally, assign each point a number and say the numbers aloud. I will diagnose blindly."

"Excellent," my friend smiles, "So, situation number one."

"Alright" I say, "Keep going."

"Now, situation number two."

"Here are the results of the diagnoses," I say. "In the first situation, the condition is excellent, the reserves of the future are good. In the second situation, the reserves for the future are seven times below critical: this is death."

My friend thought. "He had situation number two about a year ago. Precisely one year ago his five years of work began yielding results, things went uphill and serious profit appeared."

"That is to say, a bright future appeared," I note, then continue, "The situation which he accepts by inertia as misfortune was actually the only condition for saving his life. Therefore, pass along not just my greetings, and also my congratulations and best wishes for his further inner work."

I sit recalling a conversation that took place a year and half ago. The conversation was about the first signs of future catastrophe, or put correctly, salvation. After one of my lectures, I talked with a man.

"I've heard that you're interested in strange stories," he said to me. "I just want to ask you for advice and an explanation. An odd story happened to me. I took two puppies home. Asian shepherds become as enormous as bears with time; they protect flocks from wolves. These dogs never fear anything. Recently, something strange began to happen with my biggest and strongest dog. Imagine a huge dog that is afraid of every sound. I tried to bring him back to normal, but all of my attempts were in vain. I consulted with professionals about what this might be, but learned nothing."

The results of my diagnosis were shocking to him at first.

"Your dog has no future," I said, "A dog, unlike a person, feels this. Your dog feels that this is inevitable, and so is afraid."

He carefully looked at me, "In your lectures you say that dogs take on the fate of their owners."

I shrugged my my shoulders in response. "Yes, this can mean what you are suggesting, that you will die next."

He became lost in though, gazing ahead while I continued. "Of course you want to ask if it is possible to change your destiny. I can say, as usual, that this is impossible unless you change internally."

"But why should the dog die because of me?" he asked.

In response, I parted my hands. "You feed her, you are her future and the source of her happiness. If we strive towards a certain goal, we begin to resemble it. The dog internally depends on you, resembles you and takes on your destiny."

"Alright, can you explain why I must die?"

"Did you have serious problems five years ago?"

He thought and nodded, "Yes, I did."

"You're a former military officer, and you're used to managing situations, and doing so rather firmly. When you can't handle a situation, you get irritated and aggressive. Aggression, as a surface form of managing a situation, can be effective, but when it is often repeated, it passes into the subconscious. Our consciousness is linked to the body. The body is material and separate, and our consciousness also stands apart from the universe. Our feelings, on the other hand, are linked to the subconscious, where all is one. There, your desire to subjugate, dominate, and become irritated is directed at the whole universe."

"Why does the future suffer in this situation?"

"Because when a person is dissatisfied with his destiny for a long time, he kills his future. What is destiny? It is our life unfolded in time. Discontent with your destiny is discontent with your life in the past, present and future. When a person is dissatisfied with something at the conscious level, he fights and changes the situation around him; that is to say, the energy that is released during stress is transformed into active action. If discontent doesn't turn into active action to change the situation, it turns into hatred. Simply put, if we aren't able to reconcile with, change, or educate another person, we want to kill him. If we are not able to change our life, we begin to hate it. This means wishing death for your life, that is, yourself in the present and future. Is survival possible for a man who wishes death to his own future every second?"

"Do you know where discontent with destiny comes from?" I ask the man. "It begins with worshiping the future. The brighter perspective I draw for myself, the better destiny I expect, the harsher my resentment of my situation and destiny is if they differ from the ideal. It turns out that worship of the future leads to discontent with reality. Through this, there appears a resentment of the destiny linking the present and the future together, and so eventually, the loss of that very future.

On the physical level, the present and the future are very different from each other, while on the subtle plane they are one. Not long ago, doctors noticed a clear link between a human being's emotions and his illnesses. Regrets about the past typically cause hypertension, kidney problems, and often result in cancer. The seriousness of the disease is defined by the degree of regret about the past, the degree of its rejection. If there is something that I absolutely cannot accept, in my subconscious this emotion turns, becomes the urge to destroy the unacceptable object. And if I don't accept my past and my destiny, then subconsciously I want to destroy them. Tender shoots are always easier to destroy than sturdy branches, and the energy aimed at the destruction of the past begins to destroy the future. Our temporal body is shortened, destroyed, without us even suspecting.

It is paradoxical, but while slight disease may increase one's dissatisfaction with destiny, a serious, fatal illness may bring calm and acceptance of destiny. I will explain why. The first signs of a problem in the form of a slight illness may increase fear of the future, and, accordingly, dissatisfaction with destiny. When a person knows that he is doomed and has no future, his system of priorities is restored. Love towards God comes to the foreground, and the future and present move aside."

The man is silent, clenching his fingers. "How is it possible to change one's fate?"

"Through love. The more energy there is in your future, the better your destiny becomes. With a tiny future, you can have neither health, nor happiness, nor wellbeing. However, if there is a lot of love in the soul, the future will be saturated and capacious. Also, of course, one should not do things that lead to the idolization of the future."

Glancing at him, I continue. "What does a person who worships the future look like? This is a person who is constantly displeased with his loved ones, the surrounding world, and his fate. This is a person who constantly judges others, himself, and the surrounding world. This is a person who is always in a hurry, trying to bring the future closer. This is a man who persistently worries about the future and is afraid. This is a man who always feels righteous and can't accept injustice towards himself.

A miser is ready to kill anybody in order to save his money; he has a highly visible egoism of a material kind. A greedy person is unable to sacrifice. Without sacrifice, knowledge of God, that is, the Highest Truth, is unattainable. Any religion begins with the concept of sacrifice. However, egoism is not only material. Spiritual egoism is a sense of self-righteousness, the worship of justice and static ideals. A spiritual miser will never be able to sacrifice justice and righteousness for the sake of love. He will protect these values until the end. A material miser is ready to die for the sake of money, a spiritual miser for the sake of his own righteousness.

There are a few more signs of a dangerous dependence on the future. That which a person worships must be united, he can't move simultaneously towards several goals. Therefore, when a person worships the future, he has just one single version of it. The spectrum of possible events disappears, and if something threatens the single ideal version of the possible future, the person becomes dreadfully afraid of losing this future, and, accordingly, feels hatred towards the one who might take it away from him. Inflexibility, intolerance, internal cruelty; all of these qualities are the signs of a single-variant future. Next comes the loss of that very future in a form of illness and misfortune.

By the way, if a commander gives an incorrect order, he does not have the right to cancel it; otherwise his subordinates will begin to doubt him. Officers at military academies are taught this concept, and you know this. The continuous sense of self-righteousness necessary for an officer during battle is catastrophic in peacetime. For this reason, military and totalitarian regimes were always doomed to destruction and demise. The Soviet Union existed in a regime of constant preparation for war. Common people were taught to unconditionally believe the leaders of the revolution and prepare for a 'final and decisive battle.' Under socialism, this increased the worship of the future, accelerating its demise. You are not tired?" I smile, looking at my partner in conversation.

He waves his hand "no," and I continue. "There is one illusion that we have all become used to. That which we call the present doesn't actually exist. I'll explain with an example. On the physical plane we see a barn, approach it, touch it with our hand and say that it exists in the present. On the subtle plane, it is simultaneously visible in the process of being built, as it exists, and in the process of burning down and being destroyed. For us, the present is associated with the solidity of the physical form and with its movement in space. In reality, the present exists only in our conscious mind, which is linked to the physical body. The true present is the sum of the past and the future. Because the past and the future are one on the subtle plane, reality is actually their sum, and there, there is no noticeable difference between the past and the future. Simply put, concepts such as the past and the future cease to exist on the subtle level. For the Creator, the past and future do not exist; there is only the present.

When memories of the past become a greater joy than real life, this means that you live in the past and are dissatisfied with the present. Your soul is located in the place where your main positive emotion is. If your main happiness is in the past, then you subconsciously kill the present. The same thing applies to the future. If your key positive emotion is in the future, if you live for this future, then your unhappiness with the present will become even stronger. In the past or in the future you can have any possessions, money, cars, people, and communication. Love towards God exists only in the present moment. Higher positive emotions can also be found only in the present. The past and the future are associated with the surface, material world, and worshiping them leads us away from the truth and love. It is not for nothing that there is the expression, "A crazy person lives by the future; a dull-witted person lives by the past, and smart person lives by the present."

Any worship of anything in this world gives rise to attachment and then aggression. Aggression is followed by illness and destruction. The worship of surface layers, the streams of time which are the past and the future, turns into aggression towards time, and time is the main fundamental value in the universe, creating space and matter."

I become lost in thought, remembering an old conversation. It is easy to say, "Overcome dependence on the future." In actuality, this process can be extremely difficult, and without love it is simply impossible. The ability to love doesn't come instantly; learning to is a long and complicated process. The soul develops as slowly as the body. In order to lift a heavy weight, one must practice extensively and patiently. Naive ideas about the soul lead people to try lifting a 'heavy weight' immediately, and then suffering because they aren't able to do it.

At one of my lectures I received a note with the question, "How does one accept injustice?" For some people, my answer was perhaps unexpected, "Step by step." First, one needs to accept a situation, overcoming hatred and the desire for revenge while maintaining at least a drop of warmth and kind-heartedness. The next step is still acceptance, overcoming resentment, but in the soul there should be more warmth. After that, one's acceptance of a situation as a sign from above, as a warning about future troubles, while preserving love in the soul. Next, acceptance with gratitude, seeing is as salvation, and there should be even more love. Subsequently we must consider that any situation, both pleasant and unpleasant, must be seen as a means pushing us towards love and God.

My neighbor again distracts me from my thoughts. "By the way, another one of our mutual friends sends his regards. Remember, his piglets were dying? Well, now everything is fine, all of the pigs are alive."

I smile remembering my conversation with the young businessman.

"I breed pigs," he had told me. "In order to expand my business, I decided to buy a new breed of piglets. They gain weight rapidly, are good natured, and are easily trained. And now imagine how before my eyes, a healthy pig who just a minute ago frolicked and played, suddenly fell down and died within seconds. Another ran to the trough, suddenly stumbled to the ground and also died. Can this be related to me or not?"

"In my view, the relationship is most direct," I had said. "It's in your character to be dissatisfied with your destiny. One man can complain about his destiny for his entire life and still be more or less healthy, while another man will become ill. The explanation is simple. A person's soul, his innermost feelings, have huge inertia. If one person's parents and his ancestors were able to internally accept any situation and maintain goodwill, then his constant dissatisfaction with destiny will not poison his soul immediately. If a person's ancestors were atheists, and in addition immoral, resulting in a loss of love in the soul, then the person dissatisfied with his fate can acquire a very serious illness within several years. Begin by accepting any misfortunes with internal goodwill. The abasement of one's destiny and body is aimed at purifying the soul. If you want to improve your destiny, first get your soul in order. A strong person uses his energy to change a situation; a weak person wastes all of his energy on resentment and dissatisfaction.

A mistake many believers make is identifying humility with passivity. However, humility means active actions in changing oneself first, instead of the situation. Those who can conquer themselves can also conquer the enemy. For this reason, humility implies vigorous energetic activity for cultivating the soul. To an uninitiated person, this looks like external passivity. The goal of humility is not to succumb and lose heart, but to increase love in the soul."

"Why did the piglets die so suddenly?" asked the young man with curiosity.

"When the temporal body gradually decreases, the energy in the body drops and the immune system weakens. Troubles, illnesses and aging begin, and eventually death comes. When the temporal body breaks off sharply, death might come without apparent reason. The energy necessary for life simply leaves."

"What might happen to me?" the businessman asked tensely.

I shrugged. "The piglets took on the outline of your destiny. It could be a car crash, or competitors might organize your murder. Simply put, it won't be a long illness."

"Is it possible to avoid this?"

"Yes," I said. "And you know the way: through love. Determining whether the condition of your soul has changed or not is easy. The best test is the condition of your piglets. If they stop dying, this will mean that you have a chance of receiving the misfortunes and illnesses that might replace a fast and easy death. Pain pushes us towards love, particularly emotional pain, but if we stubbornly crawl toward fear, hatred and resentment it is impossible to improve our destiny. It is possible to change our destiny, but we must not resent it."

"Interesting," I think, "Only a few months have passed, yet the young businessman's results are quite good, though the situation was serious. When there is sharp, deep resentment towards one's loved ones, oneself, and destiny, the breakdown of the temporal body can subsequently cause an instantaneous loss of energy and sudden death, while the external causes of death may vary. The young man was good-natured, and it was easy for his soul to adopt the correct attitude towards destiny. However, this is just the beginning. If he decides that his troubles are behind him and doesn't seriously care for his soul, sooner or later new problems may surface."

Earlier, I would definitely have taken a look at his energy field and warned him that prayer is not a medicine to be taken when things get really bad. If a person is not willing to care for his soul, the greatest way to harm him is to protect him from misfortunes.

"He has his own destiny," I reason, "And I have mine; it is unwise and dangerous to trespass into the fate of another person." I remember the ancient saying, "A smart man gets the word and a foolish one the whip." We cannot deny a person his right to choose; otherwise we will be accountable for his mistakes. We are responsible not only for those whom we tame, but also for those whom we corrupt.

Only recently, I began to understand the words of Jesus Christ, "Give not that which is holy unto the dogs, neither cast ye your pearls before swine." (Matthew 7:6). A small child should take his first steps on his own, should fall, feel pain, and learn to walk independently. The child can only be spotted, first openly and then unnoticeably. The shorter and more discreet the assistance, the better. If a person has no desire to learn, he will neither remember nor use the knowledge he receives. Therefore, instead of accurate diagnoses and explanations regarding remaining problems and possible risks, I say just one phrase: "Congratulate him with a successful beginning." I then sit back more comfortably in the airplane chair and close my eyes.

For five or ten minutes I sit with my eyes closed, trying to doze off. However, new thoughts emerge through inertia and the theme of the future continues. Working with the future as a physical reality, one can systematically model the mechanism of impacting the future. Interestingly, the strongest impact on the present can be made by someone who is able to skillfully manage the future. The most important energy flows from there, and continuously supports the existence of the whole visible world. Affecting this flow, it is possible to change the structure of matter, cure diseases, and perform a variety of phenomena well known from the history of mankind. However, if aggression towards the future appears in the form of worry, fear, and haste, then not only the upcoming day but also the current day is destroyed.

A snowy, frosty day comes up in my memory. It was six or eight years ago. I was supposed to give a lecture in Novosibirsk, and a few days before this my friends invited me to go mountain skiing with them. The weather was gorgeous. The sun shown brightly, the temperature was about ten degrees below zero. We left for Novosibirsk early in the morning because the ride was supposed to take about seven hours. An hour after reaching the highway snow began to fall, and a strong wind blew. The visibility was fifteen or twenty meters. We talked it over and decided not to turn back. Every fifty to one hundred meters I saw a crashed car on the side of the road. Once, our car was almost rammed by a car driving in the opposite direction. At that moment the visibility was even worse.

My worries were twofold: first, the lecture was falling through, and second, we could die or get injured. In order to avoid my emotions spiraling, I lay down on the back seat, began to pray, and then fell asleep. Half an hour later, I woke up and noticed that the weather had improved, but five minutes later a strong snowfall started again. Forty minutes later I felt such weariness that I wanted to sleep once more. I lay down, began to pray, and then quietly fell asleep. The fourth time when I was weighing whether or not to lie down and pray, the driver suddenly said, "Sergei Nikolaevich, you should lie down and have a nap. When you are asleep, the weather immediately calms down; there is no wind or snow, and when you wake up, the storm starts up." I followed his advice. The weather again returned to normal and after nine hours we arrived in Novosibirsk.

What is fear and why do we need it? In ancient times, all tribes had the concept of 'taboo,' that is, certain actions were prohibited. Taboo is the next stage in evolution after fear. When an animal comes to the edge of an abyss fear arises, saving the animal from death. Fear must cause a maximum amount of discomfort in order for an animal to not commit any dangerous actions, and survive. Because the happiness and pleasure in a living being are linked to the release of energy, fear should stop energy and even cause its decline. For this reason, fear paralyses, depriving a living being of his strength. Fear is necessary for survival in life-threatening situations, but if it is present continuously the organism gets sick and dies. This is why the sheep Avicenna tied up a few meters from a wolf died after three days.

Fear is one of the first steps in adaptation to the surrounding world. An animal at the edge of an abyss will be stopped by fear and will step aside. To a small child at the edge of an abyss it is explained: this is taboo, you cannot come close to here." This is to say that at high levels of development, the fear dormant inside is complemented by a more advanced level of control and adaptation to the surrounding world.

A being with enhanced intuition is much better at adapting to the world. Understanding and intuition defend us much earlier and more efficiently than primitive fear. These abilities allow us to receive information from the future and avoid danger that doesn't yet exist in reality.

The highest levels of adaptation extend beyond the borders of the future, to the place where knowledge of what was, what is and will be in the universe resides. This knowledge comes through love towards the Creator. However, as I have already said, such knowledge is practically unavailable to people. To begin, it is necessary to learn how to interact with the future. One of the signs of a good future is an abundance of energy. You then have a feeling of exultation and experience joy unconditionally in your heart. Then any endeavors you begin go well. Your wishes come true as if by magic. Your step becomes light, and you do not feel your body. A feeling arises that all problems are manageable, and that in the future everything will be fine. You are completely comfortable with setbacks, understanding that they are needed, that they strengthen you. You react graciously to gossip, jealousy, hurt, and offense. In other words, your reliance on human opinions declines dramatically. Higher energy reduces our dependence on the outside world.

However, if a person things poorly of himself or becomes melancholy, thinking negatively about his future, he imperceptibly loses the energy and inner strength necessary for good health and life. A person who is shy, indecisive, unable to wish and dream drains his future and gradually loses it. Any desire originates from the feeling of love, so its repression is the destruction of internal energy. Many people who try to practice self-improvement begin actively repressing their desires, and then fall into depression and become ill. Often this has been observed among believers without a real understanding of what love towards God is. Unworthy desires must be contained, cultivated and transformed into higher feelings.

I remember how one day during a seminar I told my listeners something that initially sounded very strange to them, "If you want to hit a person you're arguing with, this desire must not be repressed or else this repression will cause illness and depression. Such a desire must be contained and transformed. The desire to hit another person is simply an attempt to settle a conflict in a prehistoric, primitive way. Aggression is the simplest way to manage a situation. If you learn to find common ground with other people you will be able to achieve the desired outcome without aggression. That is, aggression is a sign of our underdevelopment and inability to manage the surrounding world, just like fear.

Christianity has an enormous potential. Jesus gave humanity the commandments necessary for a person of the future. For such a person fear, hatred, melancholy are self-destructive. A person of the future is a person with higher energy. For this reason Jesus said, *"Search and you will find. Knock and the door will be opened for you." (Luke 11:9)* Everyone remembers how Apostle Peter believed his teacher, stepped out of the boat, and walked on water. However, as soon as Peter experienced fear he collapsed into the water and began to sink. His soul lost energy because fear is not compatible with higher energy. From a man of the future, he instantly turned into a man of the present.

Why did Jesus tell his disciples that it was necessary to believe and then any desires would come true? Because this is in accordance with the laws of the universe. Each fraction of a second energy flows into the universe; new time, space and matter appear. Each fraction of a second, the Creator recreates the universe over again. Energy continuously flows into our souls, which we spend on providing for the future, the present and the past. Every second, a person supports his future with this energy. Faith and hope help direct this energy into opening the future. The more energy a person gives away, the more he receives from the Creator and the wider his abilities open.

A person who despairs, who doesn't believe in himself, who represses desires and dreams, refuses to spend energy and therefore ceases to receive it. Faith in God allows us to realize the highest potential of offering love and energy, if it is unconditional. Many believe in order to receive security or health, and imperceptibly begin to pray for their health and stability.

Recently, I was told the story of a woman who was about to have a difficult operation her the brain. In the hospital she was in a room with three other women with a similar diagnosis, and they all died during surgery. This woman was an atheist, but suddenly began to pray and ask God for salvation; she survived. After this she began going to the church diligently, and dressed all in black. When she was asked whether she believed in God, she replied that she did because it was beneficial for her health. In principle, as a first step this is not bad. However, for many this is the last step and instead of faith they practice ordinary magic, which hurts the soul. Higher truths cannot be treated selfishly, a person is held liable for this.

I ponder looking at the bottomless sky through the aircraft's window. It seems so simple: give your energy, do not repress your desires, do not doubt. Why is it then that for two thousand years people have been unable to do so? Surely there is a mystery here, a profound riddle. St. Augustine said, "Love God and do whatever you want." Perhaps, this is the solution to the puzzle: people quickly learned how to do whatever they want, but to this day have not learned how to love. Love is the driver of the vehicle, and desire is the vehicle's motor. Without love desires can lead anywhere.

In continuous love towards God lie all of the Commandments written in the Old and the New Testaments. If love is lacking, it is necessary to strictly observe the Commandments, approaching them not through feelings but rather through the conscious mind.

Recently, I asked the audience at a Seminar to work on detachment from everything before the beginning of our interaction. After ten minutes their store of future did not increase, instead collapsing. I was amazed. It turns out that one must practice detachment with joy and love, while for the majority detachment is associated with loss, pain, and melancholy.

A human being has five senses, without which he is unable to live and evolve. However, in the process of its development, mankind also acquired a sixth sense. Without this sense, the preceding five can fade away. With its help, people can practice detachment and still maintain their warmth and good nature. The sixth sense is the sense of humor.

The fact that humankind's sixth sense is the sense of humor was not my discovery, it was my friend's. I myself realized recently that there is also a seventh sense, without which the existence of the other senses is impossible, and which lies at their foundation. This sense is the feeling of love.

Chapter 8

Coming in Contact with the Truth

I have always felt comfortable in the South. The sun's radiation activates the deepest protective forces of the human organism, urging us towards goodwill and love. In an aggressive state, its hard to endure the sun for a long period of time, and if this aggression towards others or oneself has passed into the subconscious a lengthy stay in the sun can result in a serious illness. Conversely, internal goodwill allows us to acquire a large amount of energy from any stressful situation. I noticed a long time ago that if a person is reluctant to sunbathe, feels dissatisfaction or is depressed, he should immediately withdraw into the shadow. Many people force themselves to sunbathe in any condition, and use lots of sunscreen.

I was curious to diagnose people who, covered with sunscreen, would lie in the sun for a long time. The level of their subtle energy begins to drop, and their reserve of future decreases. When skin reddens and aches under the sun's rays, it is a sign of protection against radiation. The cream shields the skin from burns creating an illusion of tranquility and safety, in the same way as a pill, alleviating pain, produces the impression of well-being. Interestingly, the most powerful deformations in the human aura are located near the genitalia, in the place of the first chakra. That is to say, after such sunbathing a man or a woman can develop infertility.

Just as the sun's energy can be dangerous, it is also essentially vital for every person. Once I came across interesting information in a newspaper article. Representatives from the Caucuses, living in Norilsk, which is further than the Arctic, tolerate the lack of sun better than locals, and feel more comfortable during long winters. It turns out that human beings adapt to the absence of sun with great difficulty. Solar energy accumulates in the physical and subtle energy fields and can even be transmitted to descendants.

The extremely powerful sun of the equator inhibits human development, while the sun's deficiency in the north also leads to weakening. The main centers of development have always been in the middle, in the subtropics. According to my diagnostics, one of the most energetically potent places on Earth is situated where life originated and came out onto dry land: in the eastern part of Southern Africa, adjacent to the Indian Ocean.

Still, life first appeared on a subtle level. I came to this conclusion in quite striking circumstances. It all began very well. I decided to finish my book series "Diagnostics of Karma," and complete my research. Essentially, the system was clear to me.

What is a human being? A human being is a creature with two basic instincts: the instinct of self-preservation and the instinct of procreation. Dependence on these instincts and their worship makes a person aggressive. If it becomes an end in itself, the desire to extend oneself, one's life and bloodline can lead to jealousy and resentment. If a person worships willpower, abilities, management or control, then self-preservation produces aggression which can be called pride. So, there are two opposites: jealousy and pride. Dependence on them increases aggression and brings about sickness and misfortune. For a long time, I tried to understand which of these two feelings was deeper; primary. Then I realized that on the subtle level they are one, only on the surface level are they are different.

The foundation of everything is love, and all is unified in this feeling. The smaller the amount of love and energy, the more aggressively opposites behave, and the greater their differences are. The ability to love allows us to step above any level of human happiness, and as our attachments subside, sickness and aggression depart as well.

This is what I wanted to convey to my readers in the last book, "My task is to steer you to the truth; I've helped you come in contact with it, and now you should proceed on your own. I have tried to integrate all human values in one system and state them in a few main points. It is necessary to try and detach ourselves from the human and come in contact with the Divine – the rest is not my task."

I forgot that desires and dreams can come true, and their realization may be far from what we had imagined. I wanted to help people experience the Divine and thought that through my last book I would be able to do so. However, this was an illusion. Rather than writing a book easily and quickly, I suddenly became seriously ill. This lasted for a year and a half. Only later did I realize that what I had experienced was not a disease, nor was it payback for all of the previous years of enormous overload. I had simply wanted to come into contact with the Divine, and my desire had come true. I did not suspect that I was completely unprepared for the realization of this wish. It turns out that one must be worthy of one's desires, but back then I could not imagine this.

There is a very interesting observation. If a small child says with conviction that he will be a traveler, an artist, a renowned scholar or a wealthy man, later this is proven to be true. However, if a child doesn't have dreams quite often he achieves very little in life. Many have noticed that small children are clairvoyant. They can not only feel their future, but shape it through their continuous aspiration.

What is concentration? It is a continuous transmission of emotional energy in one direction. If this process is held in the conscious mind for some time, it becomes constant. A person forgets about his goals, but the subconscious tirelessly continues its work. If a child's dreams stem from his head, from the desire to obtain comfort or improve his status, then they rarely materialize. If they originate in the depths of his soul, often contrary to common sense and the reality of the situation, then they have a very good chance of coming true. Moreover, if later the child abandons the dream, "stomps on the throat of his own song," he may pay for this with disease or death.

Particularly strong subconscious convictions are set in the period of puberty. The body enters a completely new phase: adulthood. This phase is accompanied by a huge release of energy. During this period everything, both good and bad, quickly and decisively becomes set in a person's system. If a child enters puberty with a stable dream, it is likely to come true.

I decided to finish my research and write my last book. Right after this decision, my ears began to itch for some reason. I had had this same problem before, and had gone to doctors in order to receive treatment. They had prescribed ointments and pills, but were unable to find anything. According to my diagnostics, ear problems are linked to jealousy, excessive attachment to a loved one and the surrounding world. I saw that I had problems, but for some reason I was unable to see their cause. Neither prayers nor diets helped. The itch in my ears became unbearable, and once again I decided to turn to medical specialists. I was referred to a certain professor. When I came to his office he was absent, and I was seen by his assistant. She examined me and asked in bewilderment:

"Do you have diabetes?"

"No. What exactly is going on?"

"Itchiness in the ears might be caused by a fungus, but this kind of fungus usually appears in patients with diabetes."

"There you have it!" I thought. "Again, the same theme of excessive attachment towards close ones. It looks like the book will have to be put on hold."

The assistant gave me a referral for a blood test and told me to come and see the doctor tomorrow.

Actually healing, if taken seriously, is a very dangerous thing. Many healers get diabetes, cancer, or simply die for no apparent reason. Many begin to have psychological problems and pathological personality changes. They accumulate psychological impurities from their patients for years, and then there is an eruption. "It looks as though my marathon as a healer is coming to an end," I reckoned.

In the morning I had the tests done and went to see the professor with my results. He closely examined my ears and praised his assistant:

"Yes, indeed, this is a fungus. I will prescribe ointment and it will go away."

"And what about diabetes?" I asked him timidly.

"Normal blood sugar levels are from three to six units. You have three and nine, your test results are ideal."

I bought the prescribed ointment at a pharmacy, and after its application the itching gradually began to disappear. You would think that I would have been happy, but I felt that the problem had not been solved. At the time I was on holiday in Crimea, and my friend suggested checking the biological activity of my acupuncture points. I gladly agreed. After the diagnostics, he was astounded, "A deceased person's acupuncture points work better than yours. Take care of yourself; you have absolutely no energy."

Anxiously, I tried to diagnose my dependence on instincts, and the picture looked fine. According to my diagnostics, it looked as though I was healthy, yet somehow I was dying. Within a week a tooth began hurting, then another, and one more, and after that, all my teeth started aching and falling to pieces. It hurt even to talk. Through a good reference, I got an appointment with an excellent dentist. Having examined my teeth, the dentist stated, "You have twelve disintegrated teeth. We must fill them, otherwise all of the teeth will need to be removed." I spent nine hours sitting in the dentist's chair. At the end, I dozed off even when my teeth were being drilled. "Teeth are also linked to the theme of desire, attachment and jealousy," I was thinking, "From where has this program emerged?" I remembered a conversation with a woman prosthetic doctor. She told me, "Long ago I noticed one fact. If a woman begins to have gynecological problems, a small time later her teeth start to decay. "And if the teeth are treated, her gynecological problems will worsen," I thought grimly to myself, but decided not to say this aloud.

After I had taken care of my teeth, I began to feel pain in my lower abdomen. "It seems as though the theme of attachment and jealousy is coming out more and more," I thought anxiously. "Perhaps it's time to see a specialist again." During all of this time, I had prayed and tried to overcome my subconscious jealousy. I had been incredibly jealous and dependent ever since my childhood, and I was aware of this. Therefore, as a child I suffered from furunculosis, I always had problems with relationships, and I was easily offended. Through my research I had tried to change myself and felt that I had had some success in this. Yet here I was submerged once again, and in such a way that it seemed I would be unable to crawl out.

Yet another medical professor, examining the results of an ultrasonic diagnosis, said that there was no oncology, but that there was chronic prostatitis. "Practically every man over 50 has this problem," he stated, "but you must treat it anyway."

I understood that the program of self-destruction was working in me: at first I had had a problem in the head area; then, it had slowly moved down. If I had had severe headaches or a head trauma, then most likely I would have avoided the problems with my teeth and urinary-reproductive system. But I needed my head in order to write books, so my subconscious chose the destruction of the functions that did not obstruct the fulfillment of my subconscious desire.

The subsequent treatment was not particularly successful, and the pains were very strong. "It seems that I am dying," I thought. "I just want to understand where this insurmountable attachment towards life and my beloved one has come from." Ultimately, the most important thing is to preserve love, especially before death. It's beneficial for the soul. Long ago, I noticed a curious aspect: before receiving good fortune it is necessary to suffer for it, to survive some necessary sacrifices. Having passed the test, you receive a reward. If you fail to preserve love and accept the suffering sent from above, then you are unworthy of that happiness. One of the main components of human happiness is contact with the truth. A new understanding of the world should be gained through suffering too.

Overall, after two years of continuous problems, I was able to detect the underlying structure in which the two instincts united. At first, I assigned it a working term, 'unity.' Both instincts were present in it as a single whole. Afterwards, looking through hundreds and hundreds of situations where there was aggression related to this structure, I found a fuller term, 'human love.' I then understood the words of Jesus, *"A man's enemies will be the members of his own household." (Matthew 10:36)* It turns out that the soul of each human being must make one main choice in the course of his lifetime: which unity is the most important? If unity with the Creator and love for Him is the highest happiness, then there will be development. If one's main happiness lies in unity with loved ones and the surrounding world, then there will be deterioration.

I struggled with all of my might, trying to comprehend what was happening to me. In order to feel that unity with God was more important than unity with the world, I had to go through a period of decay and death. Yet before this, there had been ten years of continuous inner work, significant experience in forgiving others and accepting any situation. Still, when I had come a bit closer to the Divine, a powerful purification had begun. What will happen to other people if they have to go through the same process? The only consolation was how difficult it is to learn something first. When the path is already walked by someone, it is much easier for others to pass through it.

So, I brought all human values together into the notion of 'unity with the world, the universe, and a beloved one.' One step was left; stepping from the human into the Divine. I wrote about this shift in the twelfth book of "Diagnostics of Karma." The book went into publication, and all of a sudden, while diagnosing I noticed that next to the structure of 'human love' there was another, deeper one. My dreams of completing the system collapsed. At that moment, I finally realized that any finalized view of the world was a halt in energy, an the end of development.

A person with weak internal energy perceives the universe as something static, unchanging and eternal. Earlier, this view was called a stationary model of the universe. With an increase of energy, a person's view of the universe begins to change. Because our energy is continuously increasing, our world paradigm should constantly change also. However, all processes in the universe are quantified; that is, progression occurs in portions. Each quant-portion is a model of the universe. This means that we can count on a temporary completeness and existence within a stable model of the world. Between portions there exists a gap, for rest. "Interesting," I thought, "Will I be able to, for at least a period of time, create a stable model of the relationship between the human and the Divine? For seventeen consecutive years now, there have been constantly changing models."

In this way there appeared a new structure which was deeper, and therefore more significant, than the phenomenon of a human being and his instincts. My usual work began again. What violations does a person dependent on this structure commit? To what extent is such a person aggressive? What emotions does he feel? Gradually, a curious picture came to light. The new structure was associated with the structures of justice and righteousness. At some point, I had an epiphany. Any human happiness and all values come together in the concept of a 'human being,' and dependence on the human 'self,' with its body and instincts, can lead to a loss of unity with the Creator, causing disease. However, it turned out that a human being is first and foremost a spiritual being, that simply duplicates in the physical body.

The security and stability of the body and its functions, the inability to be detached from material attachments, and a complete submission to human instincts, leads to illness and death. However, not only security of the body, but also security of the spirit can exist. The absolutization of spiritual needs creates an incredible sense of self-righteousness, superiority, and justness of all one's actions. Still, I noticed an interesting particularity: when dependence upon the spiritual 'self' becomes dangerous, aggression moves from the spiritual structures to the body, and the body's suffering cleanses the spiritual layers.

The way I came upon this structure was also dramatic. When I started writing the twelfth book my right shoulder began hurting unexpectedly. The pain grew and soon I could not lift my arm. My doctor friends told me that the problem was in my joints and advised various ointments. Nothing helped; the pain only increased. My relatives forced me to undergo x-ray and ultrasound tests, but doctors were unable to find anything definite; they assumed that the problem due to age-related joint change and salt deposits. However, in this case the pain should have occurred when I moved my arm, while my shoulder ached mostly at night, when I was asleep and the subconscious opened. From three to five in the morning I was unable sleep because of the intolerable pain in my shoulder.

I tried to recall whether I had experienced something similar in the past. Suddenly, I remembered: I had the same experience on a train ride to Odessa. Back then, I had posted an announcement on my website; I had wanted to teach a free course on diagnosis and self-diagnosis, because I wanted to teach everyone how to be happy. Once I became settled in this idea and began to design the system of training, I started feeling a sharp pain in my right shoulder. It felt as if a knife was lodged in my body, and I could not even lift my arm.

"The right side of the body is associated with the future," I thought. "I am doing something wrong; somehow I am mistaken." Suddenly I realized that this was related to the course. Any, even superficial diagnosis comes from my ability to see subtle fields, and for the majority of people touching these realms can be dangerous. Mentally, I retracted my decision, renounced my righteousness, and the pain in the shoulder quickly passed.

However this time, after three or four months, I could hardly move my right arm. I had a feeling that this was related to my sense of righteousness. Suddenly, a scene from the Old Testament emerged in my mind. When someone broke the Commandments, stole, lied, committed adultery, the Jews raised their right arm and cursed the offender. I felt that the pain in my shoulder blocked my sense of righteousness and the sense of the necessity of information that I had felt while writing the twelfth book. I tried to pray, attempted to overcome my feeling of righteousness, but without success. I sensed that this was linked to the book, and that when I would finish it the pain would go away.

After half a year witnessing my poor condition, my family forced me to see a renowned specialist. A young, energetic doctor of medicine examined my shoulder.

"Please, move your arm forward and then to the right."

I tried my best to lift my arm.

"You are lifting your shoulder instead of your arm," he said with concern. "I don't want to scare you, but if your arm has been practically still for half a year already, this means joint fusion. You need a joint replacement, but we do not do this type of surgery. Abroad, these kinds of operations are very expensive."

"What do I do?"

He shrugged. "Try to move the arm. Also, make a tomography scan; I must determine how far the condition has progressed."

I could not move my arm because any movement was painful. I took the tomography results to the specialist. The doctor looked at them and hmmed...

"It is written here that you have ruptured the shoulder's ligaments, and everything else is normal. However, I believe that this is the wrong interpretation."

"What do I do now?" I asked.

"Try warming pads, massages and similar therapy," responded the doctor. "After this we will meet and talk."

I realized that I had been turned down. I felt a little sorry that I had presented the doctor with cognac in the hope of better understanding. The paid consultation that I got at that institute did not differ from a free one in any way. It turned out that the several thousand rubles paid for a visit did not make a person more pleasant or attentive. Dissatisfaction with this young and confident person was growing in my soul. He mainly treated famous athletes with brilliant results, and it seemed I held no special interest for him.

"This is a great opportunity to accept an abasement of kindness and justice," I thought, and tried to treat the situation calmly and kindheartedly. Fifteen days later I finished the book. By the way, after the consultation with the specialist, for some reason I recalled a story about a certain Indian, who vowed to keep his arm up for ten years. After three months, his shoulder's joint calcified, fused, and disappeared, so that he was forced to keep his arm up for the rest of his life.

After fifteen days, I finished the book. After twenty days, the pain in my shoulder went away, after a month I could move my arm in any direction, and learned to forgive people for their unfair behavior. It was only after this that I remembered several episodes from my youth. I had had situations where I found it much easier to die than to forgive someone who had betrayed me, or abstain from judging an immoral or wrong person. It turns out that this condition stayed in my subconscious, and all of these impurities began to surface when I tried to come in contact with the Divine.

"How curious," I thought, "At some deep level, jealousy and pride merge into the single concept of human love, but even deeper, the two opposites, existing as one unit, find a new opposite. This new opposite is the human being as a spiritual being. Again, there are two competing beginnings: the body and the spirit. It turns out that the worship of instincts is closer to the topic of jealousy, and the worship of the spirit and higher consciousness gravitates towards the topic of pride. I understood why they have a saying in India, "A person's greatest enemy is thought." The inability to detach oneself from spirituality, from feelings of righteousness and justice, lead to the worship of a human being's spiritual aspects, followed by his physical aspects. That is to say, the sense of absolute righteousness and truthfulness is already a future disease."

A right person will always find a wrong one. The feeling of one's own complete rightness is transformed in the subconscious into the feeling of another person's absolute fault, and then a program destroying the guilty party takes effect. As soon as we forget that God governs every person, even one that seems guiltiest, this program of destruction becomes impossible to stop. So a human being first emerged as a spiritual being, that is at a subtle level, and only then as a physical being. Moreover, all that we call matter arose from a vacuum, that is, from structures of spatial energy.

However a sense of completeness did not come to me. Again and again, I returned to the state in which I had written the twelfth book. I had hoped to find myself a conquerer; at last my dreams were coming true. I had hoped to really help people. However, I found myself in a state of abasement, uncertainty and insecurity. This feeling of complete helplessness somehow gave warmth to my soul. I continued remembering many situations, trying to see what aggressive behavior looks like when one is dependent on the body and spirit. Finally, I came to the concept of the 'soul.' This was an even more profound and extensive level. I then realized that the soul came into existence even earlier than the spirit; That is, the soul unites the body and spirit into one whole. It looks as though life appeared together with the whole universe, in the form of the soul. Next the sprit appeared, that is life as a form of consciousness, and finally the physical aspect of life emerged.

Because the universe is holographic not just in space but also in time, any situation modulates the universe. I noticed long ago that a person thinks with emotions. So, first a feeling originates, then it becomes a thought, or rather it gets enclosed in a thought, and then action follows. That is, the whole process of development in the universe is repeated in every situation.

I remembered my feeling of complete helplessness again and again, and realized that the most dangerous state for the soul is inner security and superiority. This is because inner security is stability, that is, a blockage of energy, which leads to the loss of love towards God and unity with Him. For some reason, I recalled the words from Lermontov's poem 'The Sail', "But it [the sail] revolts, looks for tempests, and dreams in storms its peace to find!" Ultimately, internal security shields us from God; all changes and destruction come from the Creator, and creativity is also impossible without destruction and changes.

I thought about how for 17 years I had worked continuously, trying to find the causes of illness, tie all human values together into a single knot, and finally coming to that which has been known for many ages: all aspects of human happiness boil down to the person himself, and he is the body, the spirit, and the soul. The body is linked to matter, the spirit is linked to space, and the soul is linked to time. Time creates space and matter. The soul creates and nourishes the body and the spirit. If, when the body is destroyed, we keep our love for God, the body heals. If, when the spirit is destroyed, we keep our love for God, the spirit purifies and the body heals. Finally, if when the soul is destroyed and humbled we are able to keep our love for God and unity with him, then we will easily overcome the destruction of the spirit and body, and their subsequent regeneration through love. In its main aspect the soul is eternal, while its surface aspects are periodically destroyed. For this reason communication with God can only happen on the level of the soul; moreover, a clean one. Using the spirit and consciousness, which are linked to the body, it is impossible to know God. While there is at least one guilty party left on earth, while there is the slightest inner security and superiority, it is impossible to feel deep and abundant love towards God.

Jesus Christ identified himself with love. A person can call himself a son if he preserves an unbreakable internal unity with his father. In a normal situation this is a genetic, emotional unity. Jesus called himself the Son of God because in his soul there was a continuous feeling of love, which did not depend on anything. He called himself the Son of God and identified himself with love, because God is love. Therefore He said, *"He shall gain the Kingdom of Heaven if he forfeits his soul for it,"* meaning for Love.

Again I remember the events of recent years. First you see the mountaintop, and a desire appears to ascend to it. Then you begin the journey and face difficulties and challenges. Recently I saw the mountaintop; now I have comprehended the path and am ready to take it. I probably need to prepare myself for new challenges.

Chapter 9

The Tragedy of Judas

An age old question: if God controls us, then why does He not help us get rid of our sins and find the correct path straight away? Why are we unable to gain the truth? Why should we wander, commit crimes, suffer and die?

The answer did not come to me instantaneously. I observed how people tried to understand the words of Jesus Christ, and was amazed at how differently every person perceived His words. Many people try to follow the Gospel literally and superficially, and later get disappointed because this is impossible to do. Others try to penetrate deeper into the Gospel but face obvious contradictions. Some people understand nothing and defend their own opinions.

You can live an entire life near the truth and not notice it. You can see it but not understand. You can come in contact with the truth but distort it. Eventually, I figured out why so many interpretations of the New Testament exist. It all depends on a person's level of spiritual energy, in other words, on his ability to love. The panorama surrounding us is determined by the level to which we are able to ascend. I thought about this for a long time and came to a peculiar conclusion. Any truth is distorted by our imperfection, by the weakness of our soul. True understanding is impossible without love and energy. The understanding possible for a person with a higher level of development, which corresponds to his level of energy and love, can seem wild and incomprehensible for those who are still weak.

In this case fear, judgement or hatred arises as a defensive reaction. A person thinks that he is protecting and saving the truth but in actuality he is defending himself, because he is unprepared to accept a truth of a higher order. Moreover, the person subconsciously feels that knowing this truth is mortally dangerous for him. A protective mechanism, perfected by evolution throughout hundreds of millions of years, takes effect; aggressive action towards another person. This is the most primitive form of defense. Then, the truth is killed together with its bearer. For this reason, even in ancient times, people would destroy prophets and attempt to expel the truth given to them as their future salvation. Shielded from the truth, entire nations and civilizations perished. If we are ready to kill a person who tries to reveal the truth to us, what can be said about the possibility of our comprehending the Divine?

Any truth is linked to our physiology, our energy. Any comprehension is a painful change and mastery of one's own self. It is associated with fatal risk. Embracing new information often looks like a step into the arms of death. A person who is excessively attached to life and has become used to being defensive is unable to come in contact with new knowledge, and so has no future. He who worships forms of human happiness, especially spirituality, will never be able to accept its destruction. This is because any new truth destroys the familiar context of old truths.

Human spirituality is linked with the ability to modulate the future. A person who worships spirituality also worships his own future. He becomes inflexible and intolerant of any other opinions, feeling absolutely righteous, as well as being sure of the justness of all of his actions. There are always two extremes. Full protection from information is death in the future. Complete exposure to information and the inability to preserve oneself is death in the present. The new has to come and change you, but it should not destroy you. In general, people fall into two categories: those who hate the new and fear it, and those who throw themselves into the new, destroying everything around them. Only love and higher energy can unite these two opposites and help a person survive.

Often, people turning to God do not go towards love, in which the highest truth resides, but rather flounder at low levels of energy, begging in their prayers for material and spiritual benefits. An interesting story happened to me during one of my seminars. I read a note aloud in which a woman wrote about the numerous problems she had had before her trip to the seminar. Her husband had complained about her and bad-mouthed her; her mother had screamed that she wanted to sell the apartment along with her own mother. This had all started out of the blue, for no apparent reason.

"Subconsciously, you worship the future," I told her. "When a woman fixates on spirituality, in other words on rightness, fairness, and ideals, she becomes intolerant of imperfections of others, and her growing aggression is aimed primarily at her husband. Such women are more susceptible to giving birth to sick and dying children. Subconsciously, in an effort to reduce this worship of spirituality, such children do not want to study in school or develop their skills. Mentally handicapped or autistic babies may be born. This is also a mechanism for subconsciously salvaging the soul.

When you prepared to go to the Seminar, your aim towards the Divine intensified, while at the same time your inner impurities surfaced and your aggression increased. For this reason fear for the future arose in your mother, and your husband began diligently abasing your ideals, subconsciously trying to reduce your aggression. As soon as you feel that love is more important than the future, your husband's and mother's attitudes towards you will immediately change. However, understanding the importance of love mentally will not be enough. True understanding should become a feeling. This process usually takes several months."

On the second day of the seminar, I received another note from this woman. The previous evening her husband had called her and was very gentle with her, complimented her, and promised to meet her with flowers. It turns out it is also possible to change in a few hours.

After the seminar, another woman asked me an interesting question:

"I was very unwell on the first day of the seminar; my body started hurting all over, especially in the places where I was told there was a possibility of cancer. On the second day of the seminar, I was amazed to see that a birthmark had appeared on my daughter's leg. I thought that this could be a future tumor but tried to accept the situation and preserve love. At some point during the seminar, everything began swimming before my eyes. I couldn't perceive information and then I fell asleep.

When I woke up my head was spinning, and I felt ill. During the two days of the seminar I went to the church and prayed constantly. On the day after the seminar, I was stuck in traffic when a car suddenly crashed into mine. I had a concussion. The man who had nearly killed me could not explain how the accident had happened. Could you please explain what happened to me? I felt no aggression towards people. Nevertheless, both before the seminar and during the first day I felt as though I was dying. What actually happened to me?"

"You did not feel any aggression inside yourself for a very simple reason. When you hate and feel hurt by another person, this is noticeable and you register this emotion. Self-hatred, on the other hand, tends to either be ignored by people, or not seen as a danger. The aggressive impulse in our soul doesn't care who it kills: surrounding people or its bearer. Some people prefer to kill others with excessive judgment or resentment, while others kill themselves with melancholy, dissatisfaction with their destiny and bad thoughts about themselves. In the end, everybody is killing themselves. All moments in which you reject your destiny or feel dissatisfaction with your destiny and life situation became acute before a Seminar. Your soul began to clean itself of these impurities, and everything began coming up to the physical level. For this reason you felt unwell, and your daughter's mole, which could become a tumor, appeared. Severe dissatisfaction with one's destiny affects the legs. The program of self-destruction, which the soul started to get rid of, ceased to destroy the soul but began to destroy the physical body. Usually the first blow happens to the head then going lower. If you had not gone to church, trying to overcome your dependence on the future, you could have died. Since a glimpse of light had opened up, instead of dying you had a concussion."

I recalled this story when I came across yet another bestseller, called, 'The Gospel According to Judas.' I briefly looked over the book and felt that it was a crude fake. Later I realized what had happened. The initial Gospels were written by people, who despite not always understanding the material, and sometimes internally disagreeing with the information transmitted through them, nonetheless faithfully recorded the paradoxical phrases of Jesus Christ.

Scientists recognized the manuscript as genuine, but dated it as approximately 280 AD. Therefore this is not a Gospel but rather simply a person's attempt to understand why Judas had betrayed Christ. The scene of betrayal as described in earlier Gospels seems so unnatural and awkward that it is difficult to believe in Judas' betrayal. Truly, why would he have asked for thirty pieces of silver if he was in charge of the treasury, and held the donations made to the community of Jesus? If he were just a greedy man he would have disappeared with all of the money. Let us remember that Christ healed many people, so the amount of money in the treasury could have been much greater than thirty silver coins.

If Jesus and Judas had performed a show that was necessary for the exaltation of Christ, then there was no need to go and ask for thirty silver coins; it was enough to come and reveal where Jesus was and then to escape. Obviously, Judas would have never committed suicide in this case. If Judas had loved Jesus, he would have simply refused to be a traitor.

The human psyche, like the physical body, lives and evolves in accordance to certain laws. No thief, having robbed another person of valuables, would proceed to hang himself. Let's honestly admit that it's impossible to believe in Judas' selfishness and greed. There is a different mechanism behind all of this. Many people, understanding the absurdity of the hypothesis of Judas' greed, have come to the conclusion that everything was staged. They are unable to understand that the version of a show, a conspiracy, is also impossible.

Why did Christ choose to say, *"One of you will betray me?" (Matthew 26:21)* In this case betrayal is tantamount to murder. This could mean only one thing: since betrayal became possible, his disciples were unable to understand something which was most important in His teachings, despite their three years spent with Christ. The Apostles, having comprehended the secondary, were unable to grasp the primary. Those who stand by the theory of a conspiracy forget that there was another traitor, later to become Apostle Peter. He betrayed Christ not once, but three times. Did he also agree to play in the performance?

Notice that Christ was betrayed by his best students. Apostle Peter was the only one who saw the Divinity in Christ. This means that he was the most extraordinary student. Judas was an administrator in Christ's community; in other words he was the smartest, the most willful, and the most reliable person. It is impossible to believe that Christ would have entrusted money to a greedy and selfish man. However, if Christ was betrayed by his best disciples, this can only mean that it was a collective betrayal.

What did Christ's disciples lack? Let's recall everything related to the betrayal of Christ by Apostle Peter. It was Peter who hacked off the ear of one of the guards coming to take Christ, which means that he was ready to defend his Teacher and die with Him. Why then, after a short period of time, did he cowardly betray his Teacher, disowning Him? It seems as though Peter's character changed within a few hours, but this is impossible.

Let's take a look at Judas: a greedy, lowly and selfish person according to most people's unanimous opinion. If we read the Gospels attentively, we can see a completely different picture. Actually, it turns out that Judas was the most spiritual and upright disciple of Jesus Christ. It was Judas who was the most outspoken in his indignation when he saw Jesus allowing a woman to anoint his body with precious oils. It was he that said that the oils could have sold and the money given to the poor. So there was a greater willingness to take care of people in Judas' character than in the others. One's character is something which is very difficult to change, practically impossible.

There is another phenomenon which very few have ever paid attention to. All higher truths came to mankind either through enlightened recluses or through rulers and kings; that is, through individuals who held high positions in the social hierarchy. Their tremendous abilities, willpower and advanced spirituality allowed them to understand and preserve the truths of salvation. Jesus' disciples came from the lower classes. They were simple fishermen and craftsmen. Could they comprehend the greatness of that which was said by Christ? Elementary logic says that they could not. The ensuing betrayal proves this. Why then did Jesus choose for his disciples people that were totally unprepared, spiritually undeveloped? Behind this there is a deeper meaning. Why were his best disciples first to betray Him? Why was the most principled and reliable, Judas, first to betray Him?

An unexplained contradiction: Judas repented after Christ was crucified, though he had initially known the outcome of his betrayal. Moreover, if we think the Gospel through, we can understand that Judas wanted Christ's death. In this case it is completely unclear why, after his desire had come true, he hanged himself. The further we analyze the text of the Gospel, the more inconsistencies we discover. A feeling arises that reality is completely distorted. When we try to comprehend superficially there is a sense of absolute absurdity. When we try to understand profoundly, the results are even worse.

Reading the New Testament, I always wondered why the information contained in it was not ironed out, not presented in a clear picture. Gradually, I realized that behind this illogical and paradoxical form there resided a higher meaning; completely awkward and unrelated events suddenly and easily added up to a clear and unambiguous picture of what is happening. There had to be a key that tied all events together. For several decades I tried to solve this mystery, and eventually I found the key: It was the future.

I then realized why Christ had said, *"Do not be anxious about tomorrow." (Matthew 6:25)* This meant, "Do not worship the future; there are things that are more important." In order to understand why the disciples' betrayal was possible despite their obvious love and worship of Christ, we should turn to the history of Judaism.

If the core is removed from a living cell, the cell will be unable to exist and will perish. If seeds are removed from an apple and the apple is buried in the ground, neither a sprout nor a tree will ever come out of it. Any nation lives and evolves through its spiritual content. If religion, which guides people towards the laws of the universe, is lost, society and civilization will inevitably perish. For tens of millions of years people lived like animals. Strategic and tactical adaptation to the world was in their genes, in their instincts. The appearance of the world's religions brought about a rapid acceleration of development, but it became impossible to live as before.

Bacteria live indefinitely, while the human body is born, develops and dies. The more perfected the organism, the more risks it faces, and the more effort there must be for its survival and development. A usual bacterium is undying; it divides countless times, but an organism consisting of cells is mortal. Why? This is because a bacterium is open to the energy of the universe; an organism, meanwhile, is a closed system with informational links which are quite firm. A bacterium is a unified organism on a subtle level. Highly developed beings are also unified on the physical level. There are huge pluses and minuses in this physical unity. On one hand there is an acceleration of development; for its existence the organism needs a far greater amount of energy, a more active cognition of the world, and a more elaborate adaptation to the future. On the other hand, there is always a danger of it closing off, becoming encapsulated in its own problems. In this case, there is a slow degeneration of such organisms.

The Jewish nation emerged as a group of people professing monotheism, and was unified by six hundred and thirteen commandments, stemming from the Ten Commandments given to Moses.

Many civilizations and countries have died out in the last millennia, while the Jewish nation has survived because of its strong spiritual component. Governments who had at their core a pagan religion suffered one collapse after another and disappeared into nothingness. With the destruction of a nation's government, its population would transform and disappear. The organism crumbled into individual cells. The Jewish nation endured a unique situation when its population remained despite the fact that its government had disappeared. The river-bed was gone, but the river leapt flowing. This population later founded a new state. The enormous vitality of the Jewish people is primarily due to their religion. The Commandments given to Moses on Mount Sinai provided tremendous potential for survival in the future. A constant reference to the Commandments, as well as their observance, allowed them to open up the information of the universe, acquiring new energy for development.

All other nations became locked upon their own needs and did not notice that their flow of energy from the future slowly turned into a thin stream and then a tiny trickle. If there is no future, the method of self-destruction that a civilization chooses is not so important. A slow decline or a natural catastrophe, a suicidal war or a new epidemic; sooner or later something will inevitably happen.

The Jewish nation received a vaccination against loss of the future and carried it within for more than a thousand years. Constantly observing the Commandments, people saw that this brought them luck, safety and survival. The most knowledgeable, strong-willed and spiritual Jews constantly emphasized the significance of the Commandments, the importance of observing them. However, little by little people started to worship the Commandments, the information they had received. Imperceptibly they violated the fundamental precept from which all the commandments sprang forth: God is one. Worshiping only a part, it is possible to lose unity with the whole. Worshiping the Commandments turned into worshiping consciousness through which the Commandments were perceived. Worship of consciousness is worship of spirituality; a form of worshiping the future. Unknowingly, the Jews began to pray, and observe the Commandments, in order to ensure their future.

However, it is impossible to comprehend God though consciousness. The body and spirit appeared later than the soul, and are a part of it. Matter and space are part of time, and appeared after it. The soul emerged together with the universe, and only it has continual unity with God. It is possible to know God solely through the feeling of uninterrupted love. The more people worshiped their future, that is spirituality and consciousness, the more intolerant they became towards everything new; the more aggressively they behaved towards the prophets though whom new information came, and the more their sense of justice and righteousness closed them off from love.

Two thousand years ago, the country of Israel began to lose unity with the universe, closing in on itself. The organism represented by this particular human community began losing its future. Its abasement which came with Rome, whose occupation of Israel was in actuality its salvation. External abasement always forced the Jewish Nation to unite in its highest spiritual aspect. However, an imperceivable tragedy had already occurred: for the Jewish Nation the future had became more significant than love towards God. In a situation that humbled people's physical and spiritual dignity, the Jews turned not towards God and love, but towards hatred and war. He who worships the future must lose it. Israel as a country had to perish. The Temple of Jerusalem had to be razed to the ground because in it people had stopped praying to God. Instead, they worshiped the Commandments and consciousness, through which the Commandments had come.

Israel was given a chance from above. God, through His Messiah, proclaimed to the people that love was more important than spirituality and rightness. However, society had already gone deep into the worship of the future; this process had begun acquiring signs of irreversibility. It happened in such a way that those who were most spiritual, intelligent and conscious of the Commandments had turned out to be cut off from God's truth. Consciousness felt itself to be master and began build defenses against love. Those who were weakest, most unprepared, and spiritually undeveloped turned out to be closer to the truth than those who had been in the forefront. Jesus saw that it was too late. He saw that the smartest and most advanced people were already closed off from new information, and understood that they were doomed. Therefore, he chose for discipleship those for whom spirituality, knowledge and righteousness had not become the goal; those in whom the most dangerous mechanism for destroying love, consciousness and spirituality, had not yet developed. A weak, vulnerable, and simple person living at the bottom of the social ladder was more open to love than others, without which it is impossible to accept new truths. In striving for love, the very last become the first.

Now it is possible to explain why Peter betrayed Christ three times. When Peter was around Christ, love was more important for him than spirituality, consciousness and righteousness, and he was not afraid to lose his future, rushing with a sword to defend his Teacher. However, when Christ was taken away the future again triumphed, fear for his own life appeared, and love began leaving. Along with fear for the future came his betrayal.

For three years, Christ told his disciples that love was more important than the future. He and saw that they couldn't handle it, were unable to change. Why, seeing the futility of his efforts, did he keep going forward? This is because he could see much further. He saw that it was impossible to understand the higher truth immediately, but that even distorted and misunderstood, this knowledge would be kept alive through the efforts of his disciples and followers. Yes, at that time the state of Israel was about to die, but in two thousand years the whole humanity would find itself in the same situation. Perhaps by then, people would be able to come into contact with the truth and understand it, and might survive.

Judas was the smartest and most spiritual of Christ's disciples, and was therefore doomed to feel the greatest aggression when the future collapsed. Judas was unable to accept injustice or sustain love when his vision of the future crumbled. In him, the tragedy of the Jewish Nation was realized most sharply. Having lost love, Apostle Peter began saving his own life, his physical body. Judas tried to save his principles, his spiritual body, and was much more intolerant and aggressive.

For a person who worships money there are only two paths. The first path is to rise above money and no longer depend on it; this is the most difficult path. This is possible through love towards God. The second path is to become very poor, to reject money.

The same thing happens to those who worship spirituality. It is either necessary to feel that love is more important than spirituality, or to reject the spiritual and turn to the material. In the eyes of Judas, Christ, who said that wealth was dangerous, had discredited Himself by imitating the wealthy. He had allowed Himself to be anointed with precious oils, that cost huge amounts of money. Judas' image of the ideal teacher completely collapsed. "You have deceived us," Judas thought with bitterness and hatred, "and we believed you. The truth is that the body is much more important to you than spirituality and justice. Well, I will follow you in this also, but you will be filled with regret later on. If the physical and not the spiritual should become most important to me, then this will be my major principle, and money will become most important for me, even more important than your life. You must suffer for destroying our faith in you, and showing the importance of the material world."

Everything that Judas did was a demonstrative protest against the collapse of the future. He does not hide, run away or lurk. He came up to his Teacher, embraced and kissed Him, "You began to worship the body; I followed you, and so receive your reward."

Judas's epiphany came suddenly and unexpectedly. For the second time, Judas' future collapsed. Had Christ worshiping the body, he would have feared, cursed and resented. He would have used his higher abilities and gotten away from his persecutors. But Christ, knowing what awaited, calmly went to his death. Judas realized with horror that he had been mistaken: Christ did not depend on his body or the worship of material happiness in the least. This was so clear, so genuine and obvious that it required no further explanation or evidence. Judas' whole world collapsed for the second time. If his first rejection of the future's collapse transformed into aggression towards others, then this time his hatred was directed at himself.

Judas tried to return the thirty silver coins. He understood that worshiping money and material happiness was useless and pointless. The whole world crumbled in front of his eyes, both material and spiritual, and he was unable to accept this collapse. He had not yet learned how to love, and just as at first he had been doomed to betray, so later he was destined to commit suicide.

Jesus was thirty three years old then. Thirty three years later, in 66 A.D, the Jewish War began. The revolt was pointless and doomed to failure. Before this, for a period of several hundred years the Jews had been in Babylonian captivity. They had not only been killed and turned into slaves, but were forbidden to practice their own religion. What was amazing was that the Jews did not feel hatred, did not kill their captors. The more severe their abasement, the more resolutely they turned towards God with prayers and gratitude. Their captor, the mighty King Nebuchadnezzar, began losing his mind and acting like an animal. His son was eventually murdered and the mighty country broke apart. Meanwhile the Jews survived and returned to their country.

The Romans who conquered Israel were far more tolerant. Judaism was permitted, political and economic institutions were saved, and it was just necessary to recognize the power of Rome and pay taxes. However, instead of prayer, their response became hatred and revenge. The people of Israel were given a chance. There came a man who said, *"If anyone strikes you on the cheek, offer the other also; and from anyone who takes away your coat, do not withhold even your shirt" (Luke 6, 29).* People were told a great truth. Everything new and salutary comes through pain and the abasement of the existing reality. If at the moment of this pain we turn towards God, pray, and hold on to love, we gain a new future. If however we defend ourselves, hate, and resist, we lose our future along with the new truth.

I was once asked, "How about the Second World War? What would have happened if Soviet people had not stood up to defend their motherland? It is obvious to everyone that all would have been annihilated." Nobody notices the blatant difference between these two situations. The Jewish people in Babylonian captivity did not defend themselves outwardly; all of their energy went on strengthening their belief in and love for God, which was their highest protection. Soviet people were atheists and could protect themselves only externally, and for this reason they were doomed to fighting a war and the possibility of defeat.

The collapse of the imaginary power of the Soviet Union during the first months of war was simultaneously the collapse of Socialism and its ideas. People then turned towards God, and miracles began happening. The war was in fact lost, but the heroism of Soviet soldiers fortified unexplainable fortunate events and coincidences. The country that had lost the future it had worshiped, that was doomed to defeat, collapse, and destruction, acquired a new future through love, and the course of the war changed. This was what brought about the cult of personality in post-war years, that is, the recognition that socialism had serious problems in the past, present and future.

War is an event in which everyone prepares to accept the loss of his future. In order to feel that love was more important than the future, it was necessary for Russia to come to total catastrophe, experiencing defeat to its very core. This was the moment when everybody felt that the future was already lost, and that it was useless to worship it. Then people tried to strive towards God and love, and this was their salvation. An intense feeling of love flares up in moments of extreme danger, but when the trouble leaves, people calm down and again begin worshiping the material and the spiritual.

Recently, I visited Odessa and was told a curious story about sailors. On average, about thirty percent of the sailors aboard a ship believe in God, twenty percent are convinced atheists, and the rest are either impartial or serious pagans. Then a strong storm begins, with the possibility that the vessel can perish, and all one hundred percent fall on their knees and begin to pray to God, "O Lord, have mercy on us sinners. O Lord, save us!" And when a clear and calm day comes, they divide again into thirty percent believers, twenty percent atheists and so on. Everyone returns to his level of energy and ability to love.

The Jewish rebellion ended in catastrophe: Roman legions burned down Jerusalem and destroyed its inhabitants; the Temple of Solomon was razed from the face of the earth. Only one of its walls remained, now called the Wailing Wall. Israel as a State ceased to exist. Perhaps, this was a provision for the salvation of the Jewish people. Having lost the present and the future, they regained their love for God, which was the key to their further salvation.

Several decades earlier, Judas was unable to accept the collapse of the future, was unable to feel the priority of love over all else, as was true of the entire population of Israel. Nothing is accidental in the Bible. The fact that the name of the smartest and most spiritual apostle was Judas is also no accident. The tragedy of Judas was the tragedy of the entire Jewish Nation, and subsequent events proved this.

Russia has undergone a similar catastrophe. The ideas of socialism were much more important to us than love and the lives of other people, and this resulted in the death of millions. New Judases, blindly following the principles of Socialism, killed their parents, brothers, sisters and children.

Judas lives in each of us. He flounders about, trying to determine whether to worship the spiritual or the material, imperceptibly losing the feeling of love. Meanwhile, mankind is rapidly losing its future. Signs of this loss can already be seen with the naked eye. Every day, the tragedy of Judas imperceptibly repeats itself in each of us.

I look out of the window at the shining blue sky. What does the scale of wretchedness need to be for mankind to find its way back to God and love, and cease to worship tomorrow? Two thousand years ago we received a cure, our salvation. We carry it within, often without realizing, and I believe that we will be able to activate it. Only we cannot put it off. We must begin now, this very second.

Chapter 10

Telephone Consultations

Understanding means seeing the internal connections between situations and events that seem, externally, to be unrelated. Situations grow out of a single seed. They evolve, become dissimilar and unconnected on the surface, but their internal unity continues to exist. Moreover, the link between them is formed instantly, as in two photons that have flown apart. Any impact on one photon is instantly transmitted to the other at any distance. This means that the entire universe immediately reacts to any action and event, wherever it might occur.

This is particularly vivid in a person's life. Any event that happens and will happen to a person is always linked to the state of his soul. The content of his soul determines the entire series of events unfolding in his life, including the future. Genes define the development of the physical body; the soul determines the development of destiny.

I often have to explain seemingly incomprehensible situations. In truth, all of them contain deep inner meaning. I recall phone calls from friends and acquaintances, asking for help. The last call was from Israel.

"Something strange is happening to my father," an acquaintance complains. "I understand that it is probably senility due to old age, but it is still very painful and unclear."

"What has happened?" I ask.

"He has begun hating his own children. My sister and I bought him an apartment, help him financially, take care of everything, but he practically curses us and doesn't want to see us. Last time I bought him a heating plate, and he threw it out the window. I understand that doctors can set a diagnosis and prescribe medication, but would it be possible to understand what is really going on in his soul?"

"Yes, it is possible. He afraid to die. How old is he?"

"He is about eighty."

I continue. "At this age, every person prepares for death. In our subconscious, death is loss of the future. The more attached to the future we are, the more we are afraid to die. Attachment turns into hatred, and we begin subconsciously hating our future. The material embodiment of the future are our children and grandchildren. The more afraid we are of the future, the more our external demands on our children can grow."

"Can we help him?"

"By minimally, imperceptibly supporting him, you can. It would be better to demand help from him."

"He is eighty years old, what kind of help can he give us?" the woman asks, puzzled.

"His aggression towards the future and his own children turns into a program of self-destruction. His subtle energy drops, and a greater fear appears," I explain.

Recently, a woman e-mailed me a thank you letter. Her small child had constantly repeated that he wanted to die. Trying to work with him according to the recommendations in my books, she began creating problems and difficulties for him, constantly forcing him to do something: tidy up the apartment, mop the floors, play sports. Outwardly, she became strict and demanding. After some time, the child stopped thinking about death and his apathy and melancholy disappeared.

Before, I was surprised at the strange regulations in the Russian army: if a solder had nothing to do, tear off his button and make him sew it on again. To me, this was ordinary mockery; I did not see any wisdom in this approach. However, the explanation is very simple: if a soldier does nothing, his internal energy will drop and he will not be able to win in battle. For this reason, Suvorov conducted excruciating training, simulating real combat. He coined a famous saying, "Hard in training, easy in battle." In addition he forced soldiers to pray; in other words his soldiers exerted not only physical but also spiritual energy. The Army was invincible under Suvorov's leadership, although at times the enemy had far superior forces.

A person who constantly exerts energy ceases to experience fear and melancholy. However, this needs to be learned. There is the physiology of the body, and the physiology of the soul. Relationships between people can also grow, and dry up without training.

"Now let's return to your father. At the present time he is experiencing fear of death."

"That is true," the woman perks up. "He gets very upset when his friends die."

"So the more problems and chores he has, the less resentful he will be. Your help deprives him of all of his problems. His energy drops, and fear, anger at you, intensify. If you were to ask him for help and forced him to do things for you under any pretext, his anger would begin to fade. One of the main joys for older people is to be needed. This means to give energy, to take care of others, and help an any way."

Do not hesitate to request help from close ones; it is good for them. Recently, a woman asked me this question:

"Envy is cured through generosity and sacrifice. Can sacrifice become envy and greed, that is, its opposite?"

"It can," I replied. "If one only helps and sacrifices for a person, in this way corrupting him, it is possible to end up with health problems. Then, in order to survive, this good-doer will join the ranks of the greedy and envious; in other words, will stop helping others. Therefore, when sacrificing for someone, we must teach him to do the same."

Recently, I consulted a woman whose situation had reached the level of absurdity. For many years, she had helped her brothers and sisters, who had lived quite poorly. Afterwards, she began to have financial troubles and she began to provide them with less financial assistance. Then, her siblings started to call, threatening her.

"If you don't help us, we'll kill our mom," they said.

"What do I do?" asked the woman.

"Reduce the doze, like for an addict," I answered. "Your problems with money began so that you would stop corrupting your relatives. Next, health problems may appear. Furthermore, you will be surprised to notice that your character will begin to transform. Thoughts will appear such as, 'I don't believe anyone, all people are scoundrels, I must live for myself only.' For this reason, helping a greedy and selfish person is an offense."

"But why did Christ say that one should give away one's last shirt?"

"To teach a greedy and selfish person how to to give and share. The truth applies not only to you, but also to other people. By giving your energy and care you teach others to do the same. Constant, continuous help towards somebody kills them. Why should you take care of yourself when someone else provides you with ample assistance?"

There is a well-known principle: you give to me, and I will give to you. This works as the law of energy conservation. The principle is ancient, I would say, prehistoric, and it works brilliantly. However it has its own limitations: if you did not help me, I will not help you. So, this principle works well for people with low energy.

Jesus offered a new system. We must help others and take care of them constantly, without any reservation. If every person abides by this principle, he will step onto a completely new level of communication, with a very high level of energy. If, however, one person only gives, and another just consumes, this principle turns into its opposite. In this case, one person grows and evolves, and the other degenerates.

The phrase, "When asked, give the last thing you have," describes the state of a person with a high level of energy in his soul. We will all eventually achieve this state. Meanwhile, we need to help each other experience this. If a wealthy person is not willing to help a poor, starving one, is this bad? Yes. Then, shouldn't a person with a wealthy and advanced soul, who constantly sacrifices and gives, help a person with a poor soul? I personally believe that he must help, just like in the first case. In the second case, taking away material benefits is more beneficial than giving them. Asking for help and requesting it from others is necessary. Therefore Christ said, *"Knock and it shall be opened unto you." (Matthew 7:7)*

Because of our lack of development, we adopt just one polarity, attempt to adhere to it, and hope to be happy. Then, we imperceptibly go from being generous to being greedy, experiencing happiness in this moment of transition because we stop destroying the souls of others. Being selfish for some time, we begin to become sick and die, and feel our soul becoming aggressive. Then, at some point, we again try to be generous and again feel happiness while transitioning. So once more we begin to suffer from our generosity and the hatred and betrayal of those whom we help. It is in this way that we begin to think up phrases such as, "No good deed shall go unpunished." It will be this way until we understand and feel that love encompasses two polarities at the same time.

Love always contains approval and denial. Both attachment and the pain of separation are invariably present in love. When we try to escape from pain, attachment begins to kill us. God simultaneously creates and destroys the universe. God gives us life and takes it away. To understand the Creator's intentions, we must accept both. As soon as love turns into just one of the two opposites, it begins to disappear.

The elders of the Caucasus say, "Sing a sad song, but with joy in it." Contemporary western art, while attempting to express only joyful emotion, often brings just the pain of loss. A person worshiping stability, will over time begin to preach destruction. In the world one of the most stable countries in terms of economy, traditions, and rules is Japan. However, it was in this country that a sect originated the leader of which leader put the destruction of mankind as his primary objective. Another example: according to statistics, the largest number of unmotivated arsons in New York were committed by children from Orthodox Jewish families, that scrupulously respected all rules and canons. If we do not worship love, we worship stability and destruction.

I am remembering this recent telephone call when suddenly a new call interrupts my thoughts. It is my friend from Colorado. He practices various esoteric practices, teachings and techniques, and is faced with certain difficulties.

"What has happened this time?" I ask him.

He begins his story. "American scientists recently discovered that resentment affects health and makes relationships between people worse. A technique was developed to get rid of resentment. Trainings sessions were held, and people earned lots of money. What did the scientists find? When a person is resentful, this strains his facial muscles. So a person must say aloud, for example, "I am resentful of John," for example, and forcefully hit his own cheeks. Then he should remember every person he has ever resented and repeat the procedure.

I tried, and it turned out to be an incredible technique. All of my resentments really did go away! The most interesting thing was that a person at work, who had been rowdy, behaving improperly in respect to me, suddenly changed dramatically. I was amazed to see how clearly the changes in my own state influenced the behavior of others."

"Thats great," I say. "What happened next?"

"After," he paused, "Some time later my liver began to hurt. I went to a healer I knew. He took a long time diagnosing and evaluating my condition, and then said a surprising thing, 'You are in the best physical shape I have seen you in lately, but something strange has happened to you. All of your resentments have disappeared from the outside, going inside and destroying your liver. I can't help you.'"

"So what was it that happened to me?" my friend asks me.

"First, let me tell you a story," I say. "When I started practicing healing and saw that illness came from the outside, I looked for ways to cure it. Previously, I had thought that an organ became sick from inside, but when I began to see structures on a subtle level, the picture totally changed. I would see a deformation in the subtle field next to this organ, and in a year or two that organ would get sick. First, I would get rid of the deformation with my hands; then I would draw the distortion on a piece of paper and burn it. Amazingly, the diseases went away. I dreamed of creating a special medical apparatus. Once every two years you could clean your energy field, and all diseases would disappear. Mankind would be free of problems forever!

Then I saw that the same deformation can return after a while, and came to a startling conclusion. It turned out that the distortion of subtle structures could affect not just a person's health, but also his destiny and character; it could be passed on to his children and grandchildren. And most importantly, these deformations would appear when we would hate somebody or resent them. I realized that a person had to heal himself. Earlier, I would help a patient get rid of his resentment, and he would recover. Then I noticed that if one removed resentment towards others, it turned into resentment toward oneself.

Resentment is a primitive form of controlling the surrounding world. Imagine that you leave your son at home and give him certain chores; for example to wash the floors in the apartment, clean the kitchen and fit a new lock on the door. In the evening, you come home and find that nothing is done. Your son lies, thinks up excuses, and hides his eyes; in your soul there is a flare of resentment. The situation repeats itself several times, and after some time you get a stomach ulcer, then your liver begins to hurt, and later you begin to fall apart physically and notice that medication does not help. Later, problems begin at work and in your destiny, and this entire heap of difficulties has just one goal: stopping your resentment. This is because in the subconscious resentment looks like wishing the death of another person. In order for your son not to die, you become ill. There is another factor; in the subconscious there is no expiration date. Everything that enters the subconscious and settles there continues to work many years after the cause has disappeared. It is like a river; you create a new riverbed and from then on it flows in this new direction. If you direct your energy into a riverbed of resentment believe me, this will continue for a long time.

Now, lets imagine a different option: you come home, and see that your son has continued to do nothing; yet you have absolutely no resentment. However, you don't like that he is obviously lazy, and that the job has remained undone. In this case, resentment towards yourself appears, and the results are just as poor.

The question is, what can replace resentment as a form of control? To begin, let's try to understand the meaning of resentment. At first I become resentful, then I begin to threaten and to fight. In other words, I physically free my energy of dissatisfaction. So resentment is an initial threat, which pressures particular actions. So, It is possible to teach by using threats, or by instilling habits.

Let's first ask ourselves why the son hasn't installed the lock. Because he doesn't know how to, and is afraid to try. Any new task requires a huge release of energy. This can be dangerous, so a person intuitively evades overloads. This means that you need to teach your son how to insert locks, making this procedure familiar to him.

First, explain in detail how this procedure should be done, then sit down on a chair by the door and watch your child doing it. Let him insert this lock five or ten times in a row. Then go to the kitchen and ask your son to wash the floors several times and to straighten everything up. On the next day, you put the lock somewhere visible and ask your son to insert the lock and tidy up the kitchen. It will take him half an hour because this job is familiar to him now. We are controlled by our habits. First, the child will wash the floors because of fear of punishment, then in order to avoid being lectured, then because this has become his usual chore, and in the end because he likes to see the kitchen and the floors clean. When he has begun enjoying the task, this means that energy is flowing, even in abundance.

So education is essentially the formation of good habits. Interaction with any person is his education. A weak person resents; a strong person says compliments, gives gifts, looks for common ground, makes compromises and learns to change not only others but also himself. Superior control happens through the uninterrupted feeling of love in one's soul. Through this comes the energy necessary for searching, awareness and control."

"So why did my liver begin to hurt?" asks my friend.

"Your resentment turned into a program of self-destruction. You can't knock resentment out with your fists. This is a western method: solving all questions through the material level. Resentment towards yourself destroys your future, and since the liver symbolizes the future it begins to hurt, signaling approaching problems."

"And why was I fired from work?" my partner in conversation asks.

"The program of self-destruction destroys not only the body, but also destiny," I answer. "Often problems in our destiny spare us from serious diseases."

"In that case, I've got another question," said my telephone vis-à-vis, "It is about working with the subconscious. In America, there is a technique: every day you write a wish down on a piece of paper. It quickly passes into the subconscious and comes true. I began writing: "Lord, help me to love You and to forgive everybody." A few days later my mother almost had a heart attack, and later on I also felt very poorly. What might this be connected to?"

"When I realized that hatred, resentment and judgement bring forth severe illnesses, I decided to create a device that would help a person quickly overcome resentment. There is a technique which forms conditioned reflexes. On a screen, a world appears, for example 'hate,' and when you see it you get a slight electric shock. Then you see the word 'forgiveness,' and you are left in peace, then the word 'resentment,' and an electric shock once again. Next, the word 'judgement' appears, and you receive an electric shock, then the word 'love,' and you are left, once again, in peace and quiet. Imagine how much money it would be possible to make with this device." I smile. "Two or three days and all traces of cancer would disappear."

Then I looked at how this could affect a person on a subtle level. It's true that cancer could be cured, but the future would be cut off. At first I was stunned but then realized: the soul is not an instrument that can be tweaked and fine-tuned. Otherwise, soon we would begin taking pills increasing our love towards God and removing aggression. We would lose our personal impulse, aspiration towards love and God, and then the disintegration of the soul would begin. By the way, this happens to many believers who treat rituals, fasts and prayers like pills intensifying their love towards God. Judaism had transgressed in this area, and it was about this that Christ warned us."

"Imagine the following picture," I tell my friend. "A person is dying of thirst and asks for water, while you sit nearby with a bottle of water, praying, "Lord, help me feel love for another person!" The louder the dying man moans, the more intensely you pray. In order to feel love, you need to get up and give him a glass of water. This means that love cannot be begged for, but opens through assistance, care, creativity, and selflessness. Only in desperate, dead-end situations, after countless attempts, may you turn to God. It is necessary to give much more love and gratitude to God than you ask of Him. The way we treat the Creator and our parents is the same way we treat the entire world and other people. When we want to cleanse our soul, treating it like a cloth which can be washed, cleaned and ironed, the soul loses its subtlest energies together with the future."

"O.K, and what happens to those who write, 'I want to get a car as fast as possible' fifty times a day?"

"Do you know why Christ told his disciples that it is more difficult for a rich person to enter the kingdom of heaven than for a poor person?"

"Because money spoils a human being," my friend responded enthusiastically and mechanically.

"Money doesn't spoil a person; it develops him. When you have a country house, a car, an apartment and other material and spiritual possessions, you must spend a lot of energy on them, constantly subconsciously monitoring that which you own. This is development. Its just that one's main stream of energy should first go into caring for the soul, and only then into looking after material and spiritual valuables.

If you get carried away by these valuables, then while accumulating them it is possible to rob the soul and lose the future, together with all material and spiritual gains. Christ was speaking about this particular danger, never calling money an evil. After all, a good-natured wealthy person is much better than a hostile poor man. However if wealth is not supported by internal energy, it will suck the health and fortune out of a human being. If wealth begins to harm the soul, his health and descendants will pay for this.

We are used to living according to fairytales, where the poor man is smart, and the rich man is usually a fool. However the facts stubbornly demonstrate that fools do not become rich.

If a person's soul has love and energy, his wishes will come true and he will be able to buy himself a car whenever he wants without it hurting his soul. A man who inserts a program into his subconscious stating, "I want to buy a car as soon as possible," redistributes his flows of energy. He sucks energy out of the distant future and shifts it into the near future. He really does get a car, and rejoices without suspecting that over time he will pay for this with illnesses and misfortunes.

In today's America, methods of governing one's own subconscious have become very popular. Pragmatic Americans treat the subconscious as if it were a magic treasure chest from which you can take anything you would like. Recently, I was told a story of a woman who did not write anything on paper, but spent two years praying. In each prayer, she begged God to give her an apartment. Two years later she miraculously acquired an apartment, but soon afterwards her only son died. She was granted the present moment, but was deprived of the future.

What is a smile? It is a spark of energy, brimming over through joy. Americans constantly smile and teach everyone how to fulfill their desires, but at the same time are the most depressed nation in the world. The depression of these inhabitants of a 'land of the setting sun' is linked to fear for a future which has been emptied for the sake of a comfortable present."

"By the way," I address my friend, "Your mother's heart trouble and your poor health allowed you to quickly understand the dangers of such techniques. Others write notes, rejoice at fulfilled wishes but do not evolve, in effect just stealing their own future from themselves. Those who turn to God are quickly penalized for their wrongdoings and easily find a true path, living in harmony with the surrounding world."

"I understood everything," said my friend. "Thank you for the advice. I'll call you later." He hung up the telephone.

Previous telephone conversations and questions return to my memory. One woman, for example, asked, "My daughter lives in Greece. In the place she lives people like to gossip, but she doesn't want to participate in this. Is she doing the right thing or not?" Idle talk has always worked swiftly and reliably, and because human beings have formed because of communication and informational exchange, this process is necessary. Communication helps people grow, forcing them to synthesize information and to exert energy for its transmission. By the way, when a person watches TV, the opposite process occurs: there is the illusion of communication, and internal energy plummets. Therefore, it's not recommended to watch TV for long periods of time, especially for children.

However, sometimes those who gossip set self-exaltation and the abasement of others as their main aim. Every person wants to become somebody. Even animals strive to increase their status. In order to stand out as an individual, a high level of energy is needed. The sense that you're smarter, kinder, and more energetic confirms your viability and increases your chances for survival and development. However, often a person wants to gain without growth or effort. In this case, it is enough to badmouth somebody or see their faults in order to acquire a feeling that you are smarter, better and more virtuous. Week people with low energy run towards this illusion. A person with such an outlook will never have a high level of energy; this person will be a bad employee, readily betraying due to his weakness. This is because an internally weak person is dependent; he cannot maintain self-control and is easily influenced. So, the woman's daughter doesn't want to harm herself, and is probably right.

Yesterday, I wanted to gather switches of birch twigs for the Russian baths, but the trip was canceled because my friend found out that there were encephalitis ticks in the woods.

"Recently there was a scary series of events," he told me. "A man took a walk with four children in the forest, and later their arms started to numb and deaden. When they came to Moscow, it turned out that they had been bitten by encephalitis ticks. Nervous tissue began to deteriorate, the doctors said that the disease could not be treated, and the man went home to die."

"Do you know him?" I asked, hoping to help with a piece of advice at least.

"No," my friend answered. "Someone else told me the story."

"By the way, ticks do not bite just anybody. Why did this happen to this particular man? Where does he live?"

"He is from Armenia."

"Most likely he has a strong, deep dissatisfaction with his destiny, which has passed on to his children. Armenians have a a deep and profound level of spirituality. It was noted long ago that the abilities of Armenian boys were above average. However, a spiritual man can fixate on an ideal image so much that he will categorically deny the present and intensify his dissatisfaction with destiny. In other words, the more spiritual a person is, the more dissatisfaction with his destiny he can experience because it doesn't match the desired ideal; that which he expects to acquire.

After the collapse of the Soviet Union, Armenia found itself in very harsh conditions. If this person allows himself to support the deep discontent his people feel towards destiny, then disease and death for him and his descendants are just a matter of time. Diseases which come from dissatisfaction with destiny cannot be treated with traditional medicine. They contain an extremely massive and deep aggression toward oneself and the world. By the way," I say, changing the subject, "There are creatures on Earth that can withstand huge doses of radiation."

"I know," my acquaintance answers quickly, "Spiders and cockroaches."

"Well, those are insects," I smile, "They haven't yet formed the concept of discontent with destiny. How about mammals?"

He contemplates and gives up. "I don't think there are mammals like that."

"Rats," I say. "For animals, they possess an outstanding intelligence and ability to exist in the most appalling conditions. Radiation is a constant misfortune. In a time of misfortune, rats experience the flare of the inner energy necessary to overcome problems. Therefore, radiation can even be beneficial to rats. In human beings, this same process happens through love and optimism.

There was an interesting phenomenon in Chernobyl. Sterile women and impotent men who had already completely given up and feared nothing came to Chernobyl and later recovered."

I recall a recent phone call from Tashkent and the following interesting conversation.

"I am tormented by something," an acquaintance told me. "A person lied to me. Later I learned that he had betrayed and deceived many people. My friends wanted to brutally punish him for this. The decision about whether or not to do it depended on me, and I did not agree to it. Now I wonder if I did the right thing."

I thought. "When we try to solve any problem through 'Yes' or 'No,' we can make a mistake," I said. "Punishing another person may be good, or it may be evil. There are two opposite perspectives on the idea of punishment: one in Judaism and another in Christianity. Judaism dealt with the uncontrollable desire for revenge and vague notion of justice. Earlier, people had responded with aggression that depended on the depth of their resentment; could kill another human being almost without reason. In Judaism a brilliant formula appeared: the punishment should depend on the gravity of the committed offense. If the punishment is smaller then this will corrupt the offender and push him to commit similar violations. If the punishment is bigger, then it is not a punishment but a crime, for which relatives will retaliate. An overly harsh punishment for a minor crime instills fear, paralyzes a person's will and can lead to his degradation.

Let's think: what is human punishment? It is just the acceleration of Divine will. When a person lies, betrays, steals and kills, these actions are stamped into his subconscious. The consumerist program becomes fixed, and energy that should be given away is blocked. In other words a process of degeneration begins in the subconscious, and such a person and his descendants get sick and die. Punishment helps stop the process of aggressive consumption, slow down the disappearance of love and energy in the soul.

By the way, I heard that in Spain young men are put in jail for almost any reason, but just for a few days. A youngster must understand what prison is and think over whether breaking the law is worth it . In the Soviet Union and Russia time in prison was an irremovable brand, so judges, sparing the youth, ignored their violations, thus enabling the degradation of their souls. Later, however, they gave them very long sentences- from five to ten years.

There is a simple law: everything that a person sees regularly, he internally accepts and justifies; otherwise frustration with his situation would drive him crazy. A believer can live for long years in a situation that is unacceptable to him, and if possible he will try to get out of it, because internally he doesn't depend on it. If there is no faith, one can either hate or worship. Many people who spend more than a year in prison begin to grow accustomed to their situation, enjoy it, and turn into accomplished serial offenders.

So, criminal laws and human punishment must help a person return to inner harmony and the observance of the Commandments. If criminal law has other goals, then its system of punishment harms a human being, deforms his identity. In the Soviet Union, a person could get 10 years in prison or could be shot for the slightest violation, and the complete chaos that appeared after the collapse of the Soviet Union, the moral paralysis, was the result of its perverse system of goals and punishments.

For a Soviet citizen, what was most important was not obeying the commandments, but rather the construction of a bright future. Punishment stops our deviation from our goal and encourages us to move towards it. In Judaism, punishment pushed people to observe the Commandments, that is, to know God. Under Socialism punishment had the opposite aim: building a prosperous, affluent future. When our goal become a piece of bread or a piece of gold, consciousness and punishment will be violent, whatever words they are adorned with.

The system of goals under Fascism; happiness for one group of people, created mindless cruelty and inhumane laws towards others. Socialism made its major goal material wealth for everyone. These goals were not as primitively deficient as in fascism, so art and science reached a high level of development under Socialism. However, the goal was the same in essence: not knowing God, but worshiping a piece of bread. Socialism did not have the animal guise of Fascism, but the number of its victims added up to tens of millions. The more attractive a wrong idea looks, the higher risk it represents."

"Now let's return to Judaism," I reminded the woman. "Punishing your villain meant doing him a service and helping his soul, but you did not do it. Why?"

The woman reflected on my question.

"Perhaps you were stopped by the words of Jesus Christ, *'If someone strikes you on one cheek, turn to him the other also' (Luke 6:29)*?" I said.

"Maybe you are right," the woman answered.

"Let's talk about this. Do you know the law of the unity and struggle of opposites? Let's examine this law in detail. Suppose there is a certain substance. It lives and develops. At some point, its opposite should appear next to it, which denies it and struggles with it. The opposite, though different on the outside, is unified with it on the inside; it is its continuation and expansion. In this way, a parent gives birth to a child with its own character, advocating its own views, but internally carrying the parent's genes. If the child were the exact copy of his parent evolution would not happen; the new must differ from the old. While the new has not yet fortified and fully formed, it must deny the old so as to not fuse and identify with it.

Imagine that you have a car which you drive regularly. In the case of an accident, it is necessary to repair it and the person who has damaged the car must pay for your expenses. Any accident, even a minor scratch, can require repair. However, as it is always covered you do not particularly worry about it. Now imagine that it would not be possible to repair your car in the case of an accident. Where would the energy of your thoughts go? Your energy would focus on avoiding accidents. You would begin to diligently learn traffic regulations and would drive more carefully. Gradually, the energy that would go into your improvement on the road would become habit and a part of your character.

Then, having a high level of driving ability, you would be able to switch to a better car and drive at higher speeds. Here comes your lucky day; you are handed a new race car and told, "You are a professional driver so it is no longer dangerous for you to drive this car." By the way, in the case of an accident the car will be repaired, but it would be better not to count on this, rather continuing to focus on the proper driving. Any accident can be deadly at such speeds.

Christianity proposed a new model for human relationships. It is possible to punish a traitor, or it is possible to identify him in advance and avoid a situation in which he might betray you. What is the 'portrait' of a potential traitor? First, this is a person who is internally dependent. Lets remember Peter and Judas. The former's dependency had more to do with the physical body and manifested as fear for his life, and the latter depended on spirit; in other words, he feared losing his ideals. A coward always gravitates towards betrayal. A greedy and envious person is a future traitor. A person who slanders and judges others is internally very attached to the future, depending on it. This person is also a future traitor.

Everything that I have listed is a form of loss of love in the soul. The stronger a person becomes attached to spiritual and material values, the more dependent on them he becomes, the more this person is inclined to lie and betray. The seeds of this are present in each of our souls, the direction we head in and the actions with which we affirm our movement towards our goal determine what kind of individuals we will become and what sort of people would surround us.

I held consultations with the managers of businesses, who had been betrayed by their subordinates. The reason for their betrayal was usually the same. First, the manager would fully trust his staff member, then gradually lose control over the process, giving over control to him, and then he would become dependent on the employee. The subordinate would develop a feeling of superiority and disrespect towards his boss and would start deceiving and betraying him. If a manager makes himself dependent on his subordinate, he must be betrayed and deceived because dependency corrupts the human soul. Therefore, those who emphasize their dependance on their bosses, that is, flatter, please, and gratify, are also almost certain to betray.

We can constantly punish those who offend us, or we can begin to put ourselves in order and overcome our inner dependency. The law of attraction says that like attracts like. If we have a traitor around us, we also have something similar inside. This means that our internal attachment to the world has crossed a dangerous line. Through this person we are made aware of our own problems. If we get carried away by righteous punishment, we win in the present but lose in the future.

Jesus tried to change the direction of people's thoughts. At low energy levels, punishing wrongdoers is natural and necessary. At higher levels, one needs to educate oneself and the other person; In other words learn to be a person who will not be betrayed. However, Christ emphasized that He did not come to destroy the law, but to fulfill it. This meant that He did not deny punishment, but offered a superior model: a person's transformation and rise to a level where there simply aren't betrayers and betrayed.

Opposites, initially operating under the law of negation, later begin to gravitate towards one another, uniting into a single whole without fusing. In this case self-education does not cancel out punishment. The law of 'an eye for an eye' and the law of 'turning the other cheek' are no longer in conflict with each other. Forgiveness doesn't exclude punishment.

Often we are unable to punish another person because we are afraid to cause him pain. This is the level of worshiping the human soul. The greatest temptation is when our loved one obscures God. The more we become attached to our beloved, the faster we lose unity with God. Our souls stick together, and soon we are unable to inflict pain and be detached from the soul of the other person. When the pain of separation and detachment leave love, only attachment is left, which quickly starts breeding resentment, jealousy and cold-heartedness. Overcoming the worship of another person's soul, the dependency on our highest feelings, is one of the most difficult tasks. Therefore, Jesus Christ said, *"A man's enemies will be the members of his own household." (Matthew 10:36)*

Speaking of the household: when a stranger behaves inappropriately, stopping and punishing him and later terminating all communication with him is a way of helping him. However, when our beloved one acts up and misbehaves, it is necessary to go from Judaism to Christianity. Firm punishment and detachment will not help in the case. It is necessary to educate ourselves and our close one. Punishment in this situation ceases to be effective. Love, overcoming dependency, simultaneous softness and toughness; only this can bring forth real change here.

The unification of Judaism and Christianity, occurred to some extent in Islam, which appeared six centuries after Jesus Christ. There is a brilliant formula in Islam: you can punish someone who offends you, but it would be a thousand times better if you forgave him. The formula clearly shows that forgiveness is higher than punishment. It is important to understand one thing: any punishment is a means of education.

Then what about the death penalty? Can this be a means of education? It turns out that it can. If with each consecutive day, even while in prison, a criminal doesn't repent his wrongdoings, instead becoming more and more enraged at the whole world and losing his love towards God, then in this case death saves his soul by blocking this pathological process. However, if the most hardened criminal turns towards God and tries to change himself, purifying his soul, then the death penalty ceases to be an educational measure, and such a punishment can be a crime. In our Russian prisons, the idea of educating and assisting prisoners' souls has long vanished; in the Soviet Union punishment became a form of humiliating and destroying prisoners.

For a person who has lost the feeling of love in his soul, punishment of another will never be a form of education, but rather always hatred and revenge. The world is one; on the subtle level the souls of all people look like a single united soul, so it is necessary to try and change, helping even the worst offender. This is because when he dies, his soul will enter the subtle plane and will begin tainting the soul of all mankind. Not even the most perfect penalty system will be able to help until punishment becomes education, and then assistance."

"The world is united," I keep thinking, "and everything in it is interwoven. The direction you move in determines your character, your behavior and your destiny, as well as the people surrounding you and the world around you. The choice of the right path depends on you."

Chapter 11

The First Step

We will be landing at Ben Gurion Airport in about an hour. After landing, we will embark on through the familiar procedure of going through passport control- the senseless and humiliating searches that used to happen don't happen anymore. A few years ago people from Britain, France, Germany, and Russia would stand in line for hours waiting for yet another check. All of this reminded me of Soviet Russia with its meaningless actions and procedures. A person who worships an idea fails to judge reality objectively. Israelis would carefully search every passenger, fearing a mythical threat from outside, and then the problem came from inside: bombs began exploding in streets, cafes, and shops. After that, common sense was restored; foreigners were no longer searched and attention shifted to domestic affairs.

The Soviet Union also only saw enemies around itself, without realizing that the very concept of socialism is aggressive and inevitably leads to conflict and war. I recall a classical definition: politics is concentrated economics. It is true that wars begin at times of economic crisis. A lack of territory, food and energy resources push nations toward conflicts. Now, the struggle for world supremacy and energy resources is escalating. Watching what is happening, I become more and more convinced that politics is no longer just economics, it is first and foremost psychology. An incorrect worldview, a false idea, can destroy many more people than any weapon.

An interesting study was performed a few decades ago. The author was able to convincingly prove that the primary cause of the downfalls of many nations were the suicidal actions of their leaders. However, I think that the main intrigue is not even this. What is truly amazing is that all of these leaders destroyed their countries while being sure that they were saving it. As a psychologist, I was interested in why this phenomenon became possible, and whether it would be possible to draw a 'portrait' of a person who destroys his own people and country. Everywhere I saw the same picture: a ram leads a heard of sheep, showing them the way. Any leader must picture the future which the nation should strive towards. If a society begins to worship the future and depend on it, then this tendency is of course realized most brightly in the leader. The suicidal emotions and worldview of a society are realized in its leader's disastrous actions.

Nicholas II was a very kind and decent man. His softness made him dependent on others, including his wife. For this reason, he was incapable of decisive action and delayed overdue reforms. He lived in his own beautiful and spiritual world, disconnected from harsh reality.

Lenin tried to create a happy world as he imagined it, attempting to exterminate the reality that did not conform to his view of the future. However, very soon he was horrified to understand that the idea he strove towards was unrealizable and incorrect. He always spoke of dialectics but did not understand that collective thought can develop only in conjunction with individual thought. The adoption of the New Economic Policies was a catastrophe for him because it did not fit into the idea of Communism, which excluded personal property. The leader faced a tough choice: either obliterate his people and destroy Russia, or accept the collapse of his idea. We should give him credit: he chose the latter. However, he was never able to accept this internally. An inner unwillingness to live appeared, and the program of self-destruction killed him over the course of a few years.

Communism substantiated the necessity of a predominance of collective consciousness: it was quite natural that the new negated the old and struggled with it. However, on the next stage, the new had to return to the old and include it in itself. So, with time, Communism was supposed to combine collective and private property. What is collective property? It is private property increased to enormous proportion. Can a person control an entire country in the same way as his own vegetable garden? The answer is simple: he will never be able to. For more or less acceptable control over a country, it is necessary to have a very high level of energy, as well as legislative capabilities. Out of collective consciousness comes individual consciousness; it opposes the collective, fights it, and having reached a certain point either degenerates and perishes or gravitates towards the collective and merges with it.

The appearance of the idea of Communism was a natural step in the development of individual Western consciousness. The collective began opposing the material egotism of individual consciousness. However, the new, attempting to isolate itself entirely from the old, with time began dying out in the same way. The modern world is in confusion: history signed a death sentence for Socialism, but even earlier, it signed a sentence of death for Capitalism. A man with unclear goals cannot combine these two opposites, because a person's goal determines not just his resources but also the state of his soul.

The goals that Lenin worshiped and sought resided in a bright distant future. He worshiped only one side of reality, tearing opposites apart. Therefore, he had a deficiency of love in his soul and was unable to see the world as it truly was. Dying and helpless, he saw how the process of his people's extermination grew stronger, but could do nothing.

The process of worshiping the future, and the desire to unite people affected every country. The money worshiped by Capitalism separates people, making their consciousness individualistic. This is egotism of the body. On the other hand, united goals and common ideas aimed towards the future unite people, strengthening their collective consciousness. This is egotism of the spirit.

Hitler also tried to unite his countrymen, promising them a bright future. However, his system's collective consciousness did not oppose the individual and was not detached from it. Opposites must fight one another, confront each other, intensifying their internal unity through love. This is real development. In Fascism, two opposites began to fuse horrifically because it's goal was a bright future for a handful of chosen individuals.

Socialism was a natural step in the development of mankind ending in collapse because people's consciousness was unable to hold two opposites simultaneously. However, whether intentionally or unintentionally, the world community uses this experience because without collective consciousness survival becomes impossible.

Still, Communists had love in their souls and a desire to help people; for this reason, opposites did not fuse and there was progress. Fascists had only greed in their souls, and a sense of superiority. For this reason, in Fascism two opposites immediately began to fuse and destroy one other. Hitler spared no one; though aware of the collapse and demise of his country, he continued to drive tens of thousands of adolescents to war in 'youth brigades.' At the same time no remorse appeared in his soul because there was practically no love there.

Jesus told his disciples great truths, but at the time it was difficult for them to understand him. He would drive traders out of the temple, overturning tables of wares, and at the same time taught that one should not answer violence with violence. He spoke about 'love towards your neighbor' as one of the most important Commandments, and then said that 'a man's enemies are the members of his household.' People were unable to comprehend this truth, and in Christianity they began to see only one side of the coin: nonresistance, sacrifice, and love for one's close ones. However, sooner or later, this tendency had to be replaced by another one. Instead of abstinence, worship of valuables; instead of love for others, adoration and love of oneself; instead of sacrifice, consumerism. From the tenth century, a gradual growth of the opposite tendency began in Catholicism. The opposites became equal at the beginning of the Renaissance, which slowly turned into an era of degeneration. The latter tendency resulted in a severe crisis of the Catholic Church, and with it the whole of Western civilization.

Jesus loved life and was at the same time detached from it. Catholicism too, first abstained from life, and then imperceptibly began worshiping it. Worshiping life, the Western world inadvertently kneels before all of its manifestations. Women, sex, and children: all of these are symbols of life's continuity, that is, the future.

First a person worships the material world, and then the spiritual, in other words the future. After this a person should strive towards the Creator, uniting material and spiritual values. If this doesn't happen, the two opposites, failing to unite on the highest level, either destroy one another or fuse and die. The present comes from the past and gets energy for its existence and development from the future. However, when the future becomes our goal, we lose it together with the present. It is only when we understand that there are more important goals than our future that we have a chance for rebirth. Those will survive who realize that there is a more profound and meaningful happiness than loved ones, sex, family and life itself. There is a happiness much higher than a satiated and prosperous future for all people. There is a happiness that is much more significant than the satisfaction our instincts and desires.

The airplane begins to shake a little, and the crew announces that we are preparing for landing. "Israel is an interesting country," I think, "It has no constitution, no main law to define the direction in which the nation should move. It is assumed that this direction is already defined through religion." The core of Judaism are the Commandments contained in the Torah. All of them stem from the Ten Commandments given to Moses. The laws of Israel must encourage people to obey the Ten Commandments. This is where the problem begins. The criminal and civil legislation of Israel is a descendant of British justice, because England had occupied those territories earlier on. In recent decades, America began to have great influence on Israel. However, in Western legislation, a previously hidden paganism is becoming more and more apparent. The worship of material values, life, and desires imperceptibly becomes the norm, and this state clearly and consistently destroys the Jewish people, along with their faith and spirituality.

Two thousand years ago, the Israeli State ceased to exist; the form was destroyed in order to save and preserve the content. The Jewish nation stayed alive and created their state anew. Without enough love, content, that is subtle spiritual energy, begins to weaken. Then the form begins to smother its content and destroy it. Subtle spiritual energy is the future. Two thousand years ago, the form became more important than the content for Jewish people.

The true content, core, seed, DNA of the universe is love and unity with God; the material and spiritual aspects of human existence are its form. In turn, the form also divides into two opposites: its spiritual and material components. Higher energy comes with detachment from the entire world and an aspiration towards the Creator. If this impulse weakens, the next level of opposites gradually fades: the spiritual weakens and finally the material crumbles.

"It is curious," I think, "How our picture of the world changes with the soul's development and ability to love. I always felt that the teaching about the Holy Trinity contained a higher meaning, but thought that God as the Son and God as the Holy Spirit represented the tangible world and the intangible world, and God as the Father resided outside of time. It seems that I was mistaken. The tangible and intangible universe can probably be considered to be God in the form of the Son, God as the Holy Spirit exists outside of the universe and of time, and God as the Father is the unity of God the Holy Spirit and God the Son in a single whole. If we talk about the Creator and the universe he created, then in some sense we talk about two opposites and begin to see the Creator and his universe as counterparts. But God is one, and therefore the universe and that which it emerged from are merely aspects of a single and eternal Creator."

I try to comprehend this, but am not able to do so. Something similar to a neutralizing reaction takes place. When you pass from one truth into another, higher one, at some point you fall into a stupor. "So," I think, "Perhaps it's better not to touch on this topic at this time. I am not strong enough to handle this yet. With God's help someday I will be able to understand, but probably it is only possible to feel this, moreover, only through love. So, perhaps the conscious mind should be set aside."

The next day, I wake up in an excellent mood. I wonder about what kinds of problems the people attending my lecture will have. Probably like everyone; problems with the future. I walk along a green street, watching the sunlit trees. A conversation with an acquaintance comes up in my memory.

"In the nearest future, there might be problems in the whole world," I told her. "My rule is not to look into the future, but even without clairvoyance it is obvious that the situation is critical."

"I know about how you don't look into the future," she smiled, "I remember how I begged you for a couple of months to tell me about my future. For a long time you refused, and then agreed and told me I would soon divorce my husband, then re-marry and give birth to another son. I had a wonderful family, and the prediction was such shock for me that I cried for an entire day and then asked you to never predict my future again, even if I were to stand on my knees and beg. Don't you remember?"

I shrugged my shoulders, confused. "To be honest, I don't remember. By the way, how is your younger son doing?"

"Everything is fine," she smiled. "And my new husband is doing well too."

"Our destiny," I think, "Is a transition from a point A to a point B, and we can't change our predestination because it is given to us from above. However, there are different paths to the goal. Some come to it through sickness, misfortune and death, while others, who have more love, not losing but rather acquiring. For one person, in order to come to know the Divine, it is necessary to steal, rob, and betray, paying for this with the soul's emptiness and worship of the material world; then to get sick, die, and subconsciously feel that his children's unhappiness is is connected to him. Eventually, this person will acquire love. Another, observing the Commandments, will constrain his desires and aggression, going through the path of suffering faster, increasing the feeling of love. Everybody will come to love, only in different ways and through different problems. The main thing is for this feeling not to fuse with human happiness, not to become equated with it."

Recently, my friend told me an interesting story. "I was getting off the tram and saw a woman with very heavy bags. I helped her with her things, and she thanked me warmly for my assistance. At first I experienced happiness and joy, but then unexpectedly something dark began appearing in my soul. I tried to experience detachment and watch my feelings and suddenly was surprised to notice that a feeling of righteous and justice had appeared. In the eyes of others I had acted correctly; I was right. Do you know what emotion I felt next?" He asked me.

I responded by shaking my head, puzzled.

"It was the following feeling: God now loves me and will protect me."

"That is quite logical," I smiled. "When we help someone and sacrifice something, we experience a sense of physical vulnerability. If there is not enough love for God in our soul, we try to replace it with security of the spirit and the soul. Security of spirit is righteousness and justice; security of the soul is when somebody loves you and you have a feeling of superiority over someone. If our first impulse to help another person comes from love, then we don't need to rely on superiority, righteousness and stability. When a person helps demonstratively and in public, then instead of love he begins to rely on his morality and righteousness. That is why the Bible says that sacrifice should not be demonstrative."

"In Islam there is a brilliant formula," my friend said thoughtfully, "Whoever you help and sacrifice for, it is always a sacrifice to God."

"That is true. When a person sacrifices, he helps love first of all, and only after that the soul, spirit and body. By the way, do you know how criminals come about? Suppose that a person does good deeds and constantly helps others. Every time he curbs his physical happiness, he gradually becomes more and more proud of his righteousness and kindheartedness. 'I am chosen by God,' he thinks, 'I do everything correctly.' However, the more he worships his soul and spirit, the more painfully he handles the abasement of his morality and righteousness, and the more hostility he feels when he looks at people who are immoral and wrong. Then he becomes ill and suddenly, unexpectedly notices that greed begins to save him, his soul feels lighter. Indeed, his dependency on subtle spiritual aspects decreases when he plunges headfirst into the material world. Of course, later the situation will get even worse, until he learns to put love above the future, that is, above morality, kindness and justice."

I remember the problems I had with my health while writing the twelfth book. When my shoulder began to hurt and I could not understand why, I tried to look at the problem from outside. An acquaintance told me about a unique healer in the East; his treatment was very expensive but he was not a charlatan. Recently, he had cured a young man from Bekhterev's disease.

"We wanted to help our mutual friend," the acquaintance said, "And sent the healer his photograph. He looked at it and said, 'This person has cancer in the fourth stage. There is little time left, but I can help him.' The man who's photograph had been examined really did have cancer in the fourth stage, but for some reason he did not want treatment and died in a few months."

Having heard this information, I decided to do the same thing. After some time, my friend sent my photo to the East. In a few more weeks, I met with him.

"What did the healer say?" I asked.

The man thought. "Well, having looked at your picture, the first thing he said was that you were a good guy. Secondly, he said that you had serious problems with your joints."

"My shoulder?" I asked quickly.

"No, it is more in your knees. Moreover, he said that in time you will have terrible pain and will be unable to walk, and that he can cure this."

"How much would the treatment cost?" I asked. The amount was approximately equal to the price of a two-bedroom apartment in Moscow.

"This is, of course, expensive," the man said apologetically, "But I am just passing along what he said."

"Actually, everything is relative," I said. "A liver or kidney transplant costs the same. Please pass along my sincere respect and admiration of his talent. He is a true professional."

"By the way," my friend perked up, "When he treats somebody with his herbs and energy, the patient's character changes. The guy who was supposed to die from Bekhterev's disease was harsh and categorical and constantly judged people before his illness. After his recovery, I saw a remarkable change in him. His favorite expression now is, 'Just forgive him and do not take it too close to heart.'"

"I think that everything happened a little differently," I said. "After his character had changed, the disease disappeared."

"Do you think so?" the man asked with surprise.

"Now I even know it," I replied.

That evening, I came home and told my wife: "Pick three people, including me." Once she had focused on this, I began diagnosing blindly.

"The condition of the first one isn't bad," I started, "The second is a dead man, he has practically no reserve of the future, he is three times below the critical level. This person has an acute sense of righteousness and the soul's superiority. He is unable to accept betrayal and insult to his soul, so inside he still harbors serious aggression towards women. After all, the biggest pain is where the greatest pleasure is."

"How about the third person?" My wife asked with interest.

"The third person is great. He is a goodnatured and harmonious person."

Unable to restrain myself, I quickly asked, "Am I the third person?"

"No, you are the second one," my wife answered.

"Everything is coming together," I said. "Problems in the joints mean jealousy," I always explained it in this way to my patients. "If the highest feelings obscure love towards God, then the worship of them leads to aggression and the destruction of the future, because the future, subtle planes, and higher feelings are one and the same. It looks like this problem is sitting not only in me but also in my children. In order to purify my children, I must overcome my dependence on the future."

I sat and thought, "I have to frankly admit to myself that I am still unable to sustain love when I am treated unfairly, when somebody 'spits in my soul' as it might be called. This means that my system of priorities is not yet fully built. When I started writing a new book, there was an acceleration of all processes and my future problems began to actively surface in the present. As soon as I realized this my health improved dramatically.

"Hear, O Israel: The Lord is our God, the Lord alone. [5]You shall love the Lord your God with all your heart, and with all your soul, and with all your might. [6]Keep these words that I am commanding you today in your heart. [7]Recite them to your children and talk about them when you are at home and when you are away, when you lie down and when you rise. [8]Bind them as a sign on your hand, fix them as an emblem on your forehead, [9]and write them on the doorposts of your house and on your gates." (Deuteronomy 6.4-9).

A few dozen people sit in front of me. They have read my books and are acquainted with my video recordings. Every time I lecture to a prepared audience, I feel some trepidation. What if they have started feeling worse; what they are moving in the wrong direction? I instinctively worry about the future, and I need to overcome this every time. When you understand that it is not you who governs your destiny and future, you feel lighter because there is something infinitely more important than your fate and the future.

I silently look over the quiet audience. What will I see when I start diagnosis? I no longer examine the surface aura. Reserve of the future, subtle energy: these are the signs of unity with God. If this connection weakens, talking about health and wellbeing is simply impossible. "Probably the diagnosis will not be very good," a thought quickly crosses my mind. Israel now relies not on God but on the United States. Of course, it is possible to enter an alliance with the strongest country, equip submarines with nuclear missiles and an army with the latest equipment. This will give Israel a sense of confidence and superiority over everybody. The problem is that for several thousand years Israel has already been stricken with these kinds of feelings, and their efforts will not bring about anything good. You can't hide from God.

The Soviet Union also strengthened its atheistic confidence with an incredible number of tanks and airplanes, preparing for war every day. We know about how the war began. The sacrifices the Soviet people made to the scaffold of this feeling, we know also. If a country doesn't have subtle energy and a future, no military arms will help.

We cannot control our destiny. However, if we change, our destiny can be changed from above. Surface control is quite acceptable, but on the deepest level, our destiny intertwines with the destiny of the universe, and we have no right to govern it. It is necessary to know how to tell the difference between the secondary and the most important.

I look over the audience one more time. The roots of modern Western civilization are tied to Israel. If a child might die, usually his parents become ill and die first. The modern world is ill at the very least; for this reason problems for Israel are inevitable.

All of us have become acquainted with the laws of dialectics from our time in school: the law of transition of quantity into quality, the law of negation of negation, and the law of the unity and struggle of opposites. From one entity another emerges, essentially continuing the first one while at the same time denying it. This is possible when there is a high level of energy. If you simply pile up a stack of bricks, a house will not be built. Quantity will not become quality. First of all, this law applies to such a concept as energy. Energy, while structuring, generates new links and makes it possible for a new substance to appear. In other worlds, for the execution of the first law, the transition of quantity into quality, an increase in energy is necessary.

In order for the second law to be executed so that the new entity would survive, independently form, and interact with it's other half, even more energy is necessary. The law of the unity and struggle of opposites is carried out only when there is a very high level of energy. If energy is lacking, the opposites either fuse and degrade, or separate and die.

The West and East are two different ways of thinking. The material and the spiritual must not fuse, but at the same time should not lose one another. In Socialism, material and spiritual beginnings were unable to unite while preserving their integrity. The spiritual beginning began to destroy the physical, subjugating it. In Fascism the two opposites began to fuse; the physical began to destroy the spiritual and then itself.

In order for our world to survive we need an updated social system, a new philosophy in which the spiritual and physical will not fuse, instead complementing and developing one another. For this, a high level of energy is required, which we do not yet have. This is visible in people's consciousness. Their consciousness cannot hold two opposites at the same time. For them there is either right or guilty. One-sided thinking prevails everywhere.

Higher energy is beginning to come into this world. It will help to reconcile opposites. The problem is adopting this energy. People are unable to do this. Thousands of times, I have told women who are unable to have children or whose children are sick, "In order for your child to have a future he needs subtle, fine energy. This is energy received from God, the energy of love. The Divine comes when the human falls to it's knees. For the appearance of a healthy baby and the acceptance of the energy of love it is necessary to go through the abasement of the body with its instincts, of the spirit with its righteousness and sense of justice, and the soul with its feeling of security and higher feelings; attachment, warmth and stability. If, when going through the abasement of the body, spirit and soul we continue to love people with all their flaws, sustain our love for the world and ourselves, accept our fate realizing that any situation leads to love, then renewal occurs. Every person must periodically undergo this process of purification of the soul. The most dangerous thing for the soul is a sense of security and superiority; this feeling is as dangerous for the soul as it is useful for the body. However, a body that is too protected degenerates as quickly as a soul.

A state, just like a society, should periodically renew and receive new energy. For many people it is impossible to undergo the process of purification because their character interferes. Character is supported by a person's outlook. The ideology, laws of a state may prevent a person from receiving the energy of love. In this case, the state will become ill and die in the same way as a human being. Whether a civilization or a state will survive depend on what every individual thinks. Two thousand years ago, a model for the salvation and survival of our civilization was given through the teachings of Jesus Christ. For two thousand years, we have been carrying this information inside ourselves.

I contemplate and remember lines from the Bible. Love comes to a human being through the abasement of the body, spirit and soul. Abasement might come through other people. Immorality, injustice, betrayal, offense are forms of such abasement. Abasement may come in a harsher way, through illness and misfortune, and also through death.

A person who receives a new portion of love together with a new future, undergoes something like a process of resurrection. However, this resurrection is possible only when there is complete and unreserved acceptance of the loss of all human values. Betrayals from close ones, humiliation from those surrounding him, and the crucifixion itself were accepted by Christ humbly and with love. A more expansive model for saving humankind is hard to imagine. However, the human world riots and resists in the moment of its destruction, and this protest must be overcome, sustaining love.

Let's remember the main manifestations of Christ's human nature, His human shell. In the garden of Gethsemane, He was gripped by fear for His life; the body did not want to die, it resisted and protested, forcing Him to say: *"My Father, if it is possible, let this cup pass away from me." (Matthew 26:39)* Christ was often uncompromising with his disciples, sometimes even becoming irritated; in other words He too was not always able to overcome the feeling of absolute righteousness and justice. The soul's suffering is the most difficult to overcome. The ability to accept the soul's collapse, that is, love towards this world, the loss of loved ones, is the most difficult thing for a human being.

The greatest security in the world comes from energy. It is higher energy that protects us, controlling any situation. The highest energy in the universe is the energy of love. For this reason, when we are loved we experience security of the soul. When we feel that God loves us, a sense of being chosen by God appears. This is the highest positive feeling possible for a human being. However, the Divine in us is immortal and doesn't need any protection. Therefore, in order to achieve oneness with God, it is necessary to go through the total collapse of everything, including the feeling that God guides you and cares for you. If a feeling appears that God has turned away from you, left you, and the whole world around you has crumbled, and at this moment you sustain your feeling of love, this is a sure sign that unity with God has begun. Christ on the cross had a moment of melancholy; this means that this feeling will be the most difficult to handle for all of us. Through the weaknesses of Jesus Christ, the main sources of danger associated with the security of the body, spirit and soul, destroying unity with God and taking away the future, have been outlined for humankind.

"An interesting situation is developing in the world," I thought, realizing that it was time to start the lecture. "In Judaism and Christianity the main laws for the salvation of the soul and revival of the future are set out very clearly. It is quite logical to assume that criminal and civil laws must follow in this direction. However, all modern legislation originates from Roman law; from the ideals of the Ancient Greek democracy. These were pagan states, and their laws carry the energy of the pagan worship of the human body and its instincts. It was for this reason that these democracies ended quite poorly. First, there was a moral collapse; promiscuity and homosexuality, and then a physical collapse."

I shake my head, trying to brush away extraneous thoughts; it's time to start diagnostics and the lecture. I see a huge subconscious concentration on the subtle planes. It seems that accepting the abasement of the spirit and soul is impossible for the Israelites. The audience consists mostly of people who came to Israel from Russia, but I can see the extent to which the condition of the country affects their energy. How can I help them?

They will try to forgive, accept their fate, but their soul will protest. Yes, it is possible to go through every situation of the collapse of consciousness and spirit, see the highest meaning and the possibility of purification in injustice, unfairness, and disgrace; this will make the situation easier, will improve the state of the people sitting in the audience, but it will not close the problem. Energy flows through us, and it is our world paradigm that determines where the energy will go and how we will respond to the surrounding world.

For two thousand years, the Jewish people has been disgraced and persecuted all over the world, and still they have been unable to overcome a feeling of superiority and security, associated with their sense of being chosen by God. Therefore, this problem is present in our entire current civilization. The explosions and condition of a continuous war in Israel continuously shake up the sense of righteousness and security, helping to overcome it. However, so far the condition is poor. "Enough," I think, "It's time to begin the lecture."

"The universe is united," I start. "Constantly expanding, it continues to sustain its unity, which means that on the most subtle level it is a single point. The fact that the universe is expanding, ballooning, shows that new portions of time, space and matter are coming from the Source. We receive this energy, and it transforms within us on different levels. At the same time, a system of priorities must be sustained. First of all, we need to take care of the roots, then of the trunk, next the branches, and finally the leaves. If the roots are cut then for some time the tree will remain green and blooming, but it will be doomed. If the trunk is cut, the old tree will no longer exist but in its place, a new tree might grow.

So, roots symbolize unity with God and the feeling of continuous love for Him. If this unity is lost, any wealth that a person can have is doomed to disintegration. When the soul degenerates, the consciousness and body degenerate also. The Commandments contained in the Torah have as their main purpose sustaining unity with God. Now imagine: a person learns traffic regulations without which he will be unable to drive a car. He has already learned all the rules by heart and has learned to drive the car well. Suddenly, while remembering the hundreds of traffic regulations, he makes just one violation, just one! He drives in the wrong lane toward oncoming traffic. After that, all other rules will no longer be useful.

In Judaism there are 613 commandments, and they originate from Ten. Because the world is one, all Ten Commandments must originate from one, which is most important. If we do not observe the first Commandment, we will break the other nine Commandments also.

"Tell me," I address the audience, "what is the difference between sin and crime?" After a pause, I continue. " A sin is a future crime. First, a man loses his connection with God, then he begins to sin, next he commits a crime, and after that, he becomes ill and dies. A sin is a crime before God. The Commandments, given through Moses, allow everyone who follows them to preserve their future. Let's examine the Ten Commandments in this particular aspect. Please, list the Commandments for me."

After a pause, the slow process of remembering begins. "Interesting," I think, "Neither in Russia nor the Ukraine nor Israel, can anybody really remember the most important Commandments. Why then do we need religion? To thoughtlessly go to temple and beg God for various boons?"

"So, the first Commandment," I say, "States that God is one. How does this help a person survive in the future?"

The audience becomes subdued.

"Look at what happened in India. The first most powerful impulse came; Indian philosophy speaks about the Absolute Origin. Time passed, the impulse weakened; there appeared several incarnations of a single God: God the Creator, God the Destroyer, God holding the universe in balance, and so on and so forth. Again time passed, the energy decreased; even more different Gods appeared. Currently, in Hinduism there are over three hundred million pagan gods, and the country's population today is nearly a billion people.

When we feel that the Creator is one, in order to resemble Him we must compress the entire universe into a single point. Unity with the Creator is the goal of any living being's development. Is it possible to simultaneously run towards multiple goals? No, it isn't! You will simply immediately stop. Paganism doesn't allow people to enter a high level of energy. A pagan is not able to receive the high energy of the Creator, and therefore doesn't have a future. Remember the Bible:

"If you ever forget the LORD your God and follow other gods and worship and bow down to them, I testify against you today that you will surely be destroyed. Like the nations the LORD destroyed before you, so you will be destroyed for not obeying the LORD your God" (Deuteronomy 8.19-20).

Nations who worship pagan gods lose their strategic resources for survival because the highest energy is not available to them. We now see a thriving, atheistic China and a rapidly developing pagan India. However, we do not see how little is left of their old potential, which is realized in the present.

The idea of the degradation of a living being that has lost its sense of monotheism is very clearly delineated in the Old Testament, where there is the story of the fallen angel; that is Satan or the devil."

"Could you tell me please which Commandment the devil violated?" I asked. Having listened to the answers, I agreed, "Correct, the first and the second Commandments. As soon as the angel imagined that he was higher than God, it followed that there were two gods, that is, the principle of unity was broken. The violation of the first commandment automatically resulted in the violation of the second commandment: the angel turned himself, his energy, abilities and intellect into an idol. Which feelings do you think the angel experienced before he turned into the devil?"

Having listened to the answers, I again nodded. "That is correct, the sense of his own superiority and security, as well as the loss of the feeling that all is united in God. Therefore, as soon as we lose the feeling of the absolute unity of everything in the Source we call God, we acquire a sense of self-importance, superiority, and imperceptibly lose the feeling of the supreme energy of love."

I was telling the audience about how the violation of the first Commandment inevitably results in the violation of others. The first five Commandments protect us from that which is called sin, and breaking these Commandments results in crime. We break the main Commandments not so much in our behavior as in our inner state. He who cannot sustain love during the abasement of human happiness violates the first and second Commandments. He who worships material wellbeing becomes greedy and is unable to sacrifice. He who worships spiritual wellbeing becomes uncompromising, judgmental and always feels self-righteous. He who worships the human soul and highest feelings cannot endure emotional pain, betrayal and an immoral attitude towards himself. Without the feeling of love, any pain becomes unbearable; for this reason the loss of the feeling of love in the soul is the main transgression, after which negligence towards all of other Commandments follows, and the loss of the future in all of its forms.

"I wonder what will happen to us in the nearest fifteen, twenty years?" I think. "What depends on us and what doesn't? Will we be able to accept the new future? All of this is ahead of us, and for now we just need to take the first step."

A new book from the series "Man of the Future" is being prepared for publication. Its tentative title is "Educating Parents." The book's release is expected in the beginning of 2008.

The twelve books of the series "Diagnostics of Karma" focus primarily on theoretical issues. The new series, "Man of the Future" will highlight the research's practical application. How to change your character, how to raise children properly, and prepare yourself for the new future; all of this will be explained in the new series. The books will offer practical advice, experiences, real stories and answers to readers' questions.

If you wish to share your experiences in solving problems, tell your story, or ask a question, send a message to the www.lazarev.ru web site.